"Anxiety is, without doubt, the greate__ _____ and its regulation is the most challengi_____ ment in marital happiness. The autl_____ dilemma with deep and profound clarity and its resolution in clear instructions and exercises. Every couple who follows this path will end up in the kingdom of marital bliss. As the authors say, practice leads to permanence. I recommend this book not only to all couples, but also to all couples therapists. It will make their work with couples less anxious!"

—Harville Hendrix, PhD, author of *Getting the Love You Want* and coauthor of *Receiving Love* with Helen LaKelly Hunt, PhD

"*Anxious in Love* brings help for anxiety disorders into new territory, revealing how it can affect both partners in a relationship and endanger the well-being of their connection. In a compassionate, step-by-step strategy, the anxiety disorder is first managed, and then mastered using both behavioral and psychological tools. Ultimately these practices are woven into an effective program for couples to use—one that empowers both partners to calm the inner and outer effects of anxiety on their relationship and maintain a quality connection. *Anxious in Love* is an invaluable resource and guide for anyone suffering from an anxiety disorder or anyone in a relationship with someone who suffers from anxiety."

—Eleanor Payson, LMSW, author of *The Wizard of Oz and Other Narcissists*

"Anxiety, phobias, compulsions, and social avoidance can erode and even destroy relationships. *Anxious in Love* gives you the tools to decrease, manage, and even eliminate your excessive anxiety (or to understand your anxious partner). After reading the simple but powerful methods in the book, I am confident you'll be anxious to try them and will feel better right away."

—Bill O'Hanlon, author of *The Change Your Life Book* and *Rewriting Love Stories*

"Above all, therapists should not overlook the great advantage of prescribing *Anxious in Love* as a workbook for patients to use in tandem with ongoing psychotherapy. Its use will help patients get more out of their therapy by promoting self-awareness and self-reliance, as well as expanding self-care for stabilization, boundary development, and affect management."

—Claire Frederick, MD, coauthor of *Inner Strengths* and *Healing the Divided Self*

"This book is written primarily for people suffering from anxiety, but also for their partners.... There is a wide range of specific exercises for readers to try, so they can find what works best to reduce the overall anxiety level, recognize emotional and physical triggering experiences so the anxious reaction can be prevented, and perhaps most importantly, to learn to be calm, not merely avoiding the anxiety.... The authors bring multiple human examples from their decades of clinical experience, simple assessments, and many practical exercises. They create a light and reassuring mood with a genuine concern to assist healing.... Anyone suffering from the potentially crippling fallout from any of the potentially crippling experiences of anxiety is likely to have significant benefit from actively engaging with this book."

—Robert B. McNeilly, MBBS, CET, director of the Milton H. Erickson Institute of Tasmania

ANXIOUS

in
LOVE

how to manage your anxiety,
reduce conflict & reconnect
with your partner

CAROLYN DAITCH, PhD
LISSAH LORBERBAUM, MA

New Harbinger Publications, Inc.

Distributed in Canada by Raincoast Books

Copyright © 2012 by Carolyn Daitch and Lissah Lorberbaum
New Harbinger Publications, Inc.
5674 Shattuck Avenue
Oakland, CA 94609
www.newharbinger.com

Cover design by Amy Shoup; Text design by Michele Waters-Kermes;

Acquired by Tesilya Hanauer; Edited by Nelda Street

Library of Congress Cataloging-in-Publication Data
Daitch, Carolyn.
  Anxious in love : how to manage your anxiety, reduce conflict, and reconnect with your partner / Carolyn Daitch and Lissah Lorberbaum.
     p. cm.
  Includes bibliographical references.
  ISBN 978-1-60882-231-7 (pbk. : alk. paper) -- ISBN 978-1-60882-232-4 (pdf e-book) -- ISBN 978-1-60882-233-1 (epub)
  1. Anxiety. 2. Interpersonal relations. 3. Couples--Psychology. I. Lorberbaum, Lissah. II. Title.
  BF575.A6D32 2012
  152.4'6--dc23

                    2012024165

Printed in the United States of America

22   21   20

15   14   13   12   11   10   9   8

Contents

Acknowledgments

Four weeks before the manuscript for this book was due to be submitted to the publisher, I was diagnosed with breast cancer. Juggling maintaining a full private practice with teaching and writing a book is a lot to manage in my generally busy life. With cancer and the requisite medical appointments and procedures thrown into the mix, I could barely keep up. How fortunate that I had an amazing team of collaborators, Lissah Lorberbaum and Cindy Barrilleaux, who surrounded me with love and support, and who put in extra hours of work so that we could meet our deadline.

I am deeply grateful to my writing partner, Lissah Lorberbaum, for her goodwill, her keen and organized mind, and particularly her excellent memory. Working with our editor, Cindy Barrilleaux, was a pure delight. We laughed and buoyed each other's spirits as we put finishing touches on the chapters. This project benefited tremendously from Cindy's astute editorial judgment, feedback, wisdom, experience, and consistent encouragement.

I have been fortunate to work with the amazing team at New Harbinger. From the inception of the book, they have been supportive and enthusiastic about the project. Thanks and sincere appreciation to Angela Autry Gorden, Tesilya Hanauer, Nicola Skidmore, Jess Beebe, and Nelda Street. I also want to acknowledge the colleagues and friends I called on to read sections of the book: Catherine Herzog, Sabine Chrisman, and Judith Schmidt. Thanks to Harville Hendrix for his keen insights and willingness to inspire and exchange ideas with me. And thanks to Marcia Ferstenfeld, my fellow Imago therapist, for sharing her thoughts so graciously. I am especially indebted to Gail Berkove and Jonathan Falk, who generously invested their time to pore over sections of the book.

As always, my trusted assistant, Cathy Hirsch; my ever-patient husband, Russ Graham; and my understanding son, Daniel Rubin, create my solid inner circle. I so appreciate their support as I travel on this rewarding career path.

—Carolyn Daitch

First I would like to thank you, the reader. It's the collective movement toward healing and growth that makes books such as this one possible. Years ago I made the decision to actively pursue a path of personal growth, healing, and recovery. It's an honor to share a path of recovery with those who seek not just to alleviate anxiety, but also to enrich the quality of day-to-day, moment-to-moment experience and enhance the depth of personal relationships.

Regarding some of the personal relationships that continue to enhance my life, I cannot give enough thanks to Carolyn Daitch for her friendship, mentorship, and care. It's an honor for me to arrive at a point in my life where Carolyn is not only a mentor, but a colleague as well. Thanks to Carolyn for the journey we continue to take together. Thanks also to the friends and family who share their hearts with me on a daily basis, and to the clients I see who do the same.

I would also like to express my gratitude to those who have given their time and care to the pages of this book. It has been a treat to work with the team at New Harbinger. Thanks especially to Angela Autry Gorden, Tesilya Hanauer, Nicola Skidmore, Jess Beebe, and Nelda Street for their active involvement throughout the writing process and continued enthusiasm for the project. Cindy Barrilleaux's contribution has been invaluable as well: poring over every page with her keen eyes, making sure that every word counts.

Finally, I want to thank Carolyn's son, Daniel Rubin, matchmaker extraordinaire. I still remember sitting in the coffee shop with Daniel in Oberlin, Ohio, when he suggested that his mother and I would make a great team. Years later, I'm thrilled to get the opportunity to canonize the following sentiment: *You were right, as usual.*

—Lissah Lorberbaum

Introduction

"I don't know what to do," Jenny confided to her sister. "Scott and I had a huge argument last night—again. This time he was angry that I wouldn't go to his college reunion, even though he knows I can't stand being around strangers and I'm terrified of flying. Scott just doesn't *get* me anymore."

Nicole put down her coffee cup and reached for her younger sister's hand. "You know, Jen, you've always worried a lot. Lots of times, you worry about things I wouldn't give a second thought to. I think that's one of the main reasons I'm sometimes impatient with you. Do you think your worrying is hurting your marriage?"

"I don't know. Maybe. Like I said, he just doesn't understand me," Jenny responded. "Nowadays I wonder how we ever got together in the first place; we're never on the same page. Whenever I'm anxious and go to him for support, he says that I'm just blowing everything out of proportion and that I worry too much. He says I should just relax. I know he thinks he's helping me when he says that, but he's not; it makes me feel like I'm unreasonable and needy, and like he doesn't care. I *can't* just put my worries out of my mind and relax. It's not that simple."

In our years of treating clients with chronic anxiety, we've seen the hurt and frustration that chronic anxiety can cause partners in an intimate relationship. All relationships are challenging, but when one partner suffers from severe anxiety, the challenges are intensified. Over time, anxiety can strain even the most loving relationship, damaging trust and intimacy. Both partners begin to feel that the other "just doesn't get it." And this may be true, because when one partner has an anxiety disorder and the other does not, each has a fundamentally different experience of life. These different experiences can create an ever-widening chasm.

If you suffer from anxiety, you know that the experience can be very isolating: worry may occupy your thoughts almost constantly, causing you to belabor every decision and to approach each moment in fear that disaster lies just around the corner. Or you may become flooded with a panic so overwhelming and unrelenting that neither you nor your partner can cause it to subside. You may not be able to imagine your anxiety being as hard on your partner as it is on you, but it can be. Anxiety can harm your partner—and your intimate relationship—just as much as it hurts you individually.

The sense of mutual connection, fueled by shared understanding and caring, is a fundamental ingredient of intimate relationships. Your anxiety can chip away at this sense of connection. As time passes, your frustration, alienation, and isolation may grow. And, unable to assuage your anxiety, your partner may become more and more frustrated too. As your conflict intensifies, so does your "disconnect." You both may feel that although you are talking, you are not communicating. What's worse, you may see no way around the frustration that each of you experiences. Like Jenny, you may remember the mutual care and connection that you once treasured in your relationship and fear that this connection is forever lost.

While it's natural to want your partner to "fix" your anxiety when it arises, and to feel disappointed when your partner doesn't do this, the reality is that *you* are the only one with the power to overcome your anxiety. As hard as it may be to accept, you have the power—and the responsibility—to do the heavy lifting in that process. However, you're not on this journey alone. The purpose of this book is to provide you with a variety of techniques to help you ease your anxiety, reduce conflict, and foster connection with your partner.

Gaining a better understanding of the rifts in your relationship, and learning specific techniques and skills that will help you enhance your sense of connection, begins with learning more effective ways to manage your own anxiety. The exercises in part 1, "Dialing Down Distress," provide you with tools to calm your anxiety so that your once-insurmountable fears can begin to subside.

Once you are able to modulate your anxiety levels, you are ready to turn your attention to your relationship. In parts 2 and 3, you will learn how to improve your communication and strengthen your sense of connection with your partner. The first step in this process is to understand the dynamics that occur when one partner in a relationship has an anxiety disorder. Then you will learn the identifiable patterns of communication and behavior that can damage trust and intimacy over time. Parts 2 and 3 provide you with tools to break these patterns and create new ways of interacting that will foster the deep connection and bond you both desire.

How to Use This Book

This book is written primarily for you, the partner who suffers from anxiety. Each chapter offers you insight about anxiety and concrete tools to help you manage it. Because the chapters and techniques build on one another, you'll get the most from the book by reading the chapters sequentially. And because you are not simply reading a book but are also engaging in a process of healing and change, you need to take enough time with each chapter to become comfortable with the exercises and the new skills you gain from them. It's not to your advantage to whiz through this book at breakneck speed.

Obviously then, it's important to practice the techniques in each chapter, even if they don't come naturally at first. Learning these techniques is a bit like learning the guitar: You don't learn all the chords in one day. You learn one chord at a time, gaining skill over time through repeated practice. So rather than just try each exercise once, practice the techniques in each chapter often. This is how you can build and solidify a repertoire of skills and techniques for permanently reducing your anxiety. After you've read the book, keep it handy so that you can refer back to any of the exercises whenever you need a refresher.

If you are the nonanxious partner, this book can help you better understand your partner's anxiety and the ways that you can improve the communication patterns in your relationship. Of course, you can gain the most by reading the entire book. Part 1 gives you greater insight into the specific challenges that your partner faces in living with an anxiety disorder, and it details the new tools and techniques your partner is using to de-escalate her anxiety. It's especially important that you understand the time-out technique for de-escalating anxiety that your partner will be using, which is presented in chapter 2. Time-outs are the foundation of all the anxiety-reducing exercises your partner will use in the future to lessen anxiety. It's essential that you understand the purpose and benefit of the time-outs so that you can encourage your partner's progress. This technique will also de-escalate the conflict in your relationship, so you can benefit from practicing time-outs too.

Your anxious partner's growth and change is only half the solution. Parts 2 and 3 provide exercises specifically designed to deepen your partnership so that it becomes a relationship characterized by trust, respect, and healthy interdependence. By doing the exercises in these parts as they apply to you, you can further the process that your partner is advancing and gain a deeply satisfying relationship. Please note that appendices A and B are written specifically for you, the nonanxious partner. They provide tips and strategies to help you resolve the misunderstandings that can arise when your partner is suffering from anxiety.

Anxiety affects every aspect of life, replacing fulfillment and satisfaction with misery. Yet your anxiety can be a catalyst for growth. The seeds of change for you and your partnership are contained in the pages that follow. It is our hope that as you embark on this journey of recovery and transformation, you are looking forward to freedom from anxiety. The fruits of your labor toward that end are boundless. There is no time like the present to begin.

part 1

DIALING DOWN DISTRESS

chapter 1

Understanding Your Anxiety

We've all experienced *fear*: a strong physical and psychological response to perceived danger. We wouldn't be human if we didn't. We've all experienced *anxiety* as well: a state of physical and psychological agitation typically accompanied by uneasy feelings; physical discomfort; worried, obsessive, or catastrophic thoughts; and rigid and avoidant behaviors. The ability to experience fear and anxiety is, in fact, necessary for our survival and can serve us in countless ways. Fear and anxiety help alert us to the possibility that some aspect of our well-being might be in jeopardy. The experience of fear and anxiety then helps mobilize our minds and bodies to determine if a threat is present and helps protect us should a threat exist.

For example, the surge of fear you experience as you register that the car on the road in front of you has stopped abruptly helps your body mobilize to slam on the brakes. Your fear of having a car accident, motivated by your desire to protect yourself and others from harm, helps you mobilize your resources in an attempt to avoid a collision. Similarly, the anxiety you experience as you anticipate an upcoming annual review with your supervisor might motivate you to enhance your job performance. The anxiety created by the possibility of receiving a poor review spurs you into action so that you can maintain your job security. Thus the ability to experience fear and anxiety is very adaptive.

However, problems can arise when the level of fear or anxiety that you experience is disproportionate to the situation that you are currently encountering. In other words, it's important that your degree of fear or anxiety is adaptive to the situation at hand. If your anxiety or fear is too high, it no longer helps you respond optimally to your situation or environment. In fact, the excessive fear and anxiety become a hindrance. For example, if knowing about an upcoming job-performance review causes you to become so flustered with mounting worry during the preceding weeks that your work productivity decreases, then anxiety becomes a hindrance rather than an aid. Or if, *every* time you attempted to drive, you experienced the same surge of fear that once helped you avoid having a car accident, you would certainly find driving so stressful that you would avoid it. This maladaptive response could lead you to depend on your partner to take over the driving entirely, which could put a strain on the relationship. The same degree of fear that can save your life in one moment, when sustained, can greatly impede your life and become maladaptive. So rather than look at anxiety as either good or bad, it's more helpful to ask yourself, *Does my anxiety interfere with my functioning or satisfaction with my life and my relationship with my partner? Might an objective observer, or even my partner, think that the degree of anxiety I am experiencing is excessive relative to the situation that triggers it?* If you answered yes to either or both of these questions, this chapter will help you better identify the types of anxiety that you experience.

If you are reading this book because you suffer from anxiety, it's possible that you have an anxiety disorder. However, you don't need to have a diagnosed anxiety disorder for anxiety to negatively affect your life. The distinction is a matter of degree: the extent to which your anxiety interferes with your full functioning and enjoyment of life, including your enjoyment of your relationship. Common to all expressions of chronic anxiety is a pervasive sense of fear and uneasiness that interferes with feeling that you are okay. Regardless of the type of anxiety you experience, this pervasive sense of "disease" takes a toll on your body, your mind, and your relationships with the most significant people in your life.

Let's first look at common responses you might have to life situations if you are an anxiety-prone person. (Remember, being anxiety prone doesn't necessarily mean that you have an anxiety disorder.) We will examine the toll that these response patterns can exact on your quality of life—and the quality of your relationship. Next we will introduce the six anxiety disorders and the types of fears and anxieties that characterize each. At the end of the chapter are two questionnaires to help you assess the degree to which anxiety affects your life and your relationship with your spouse or partner. Knowledge brings self-understanding. Being able to identify your anxiety is the first step in overcoming its grip and transforming your relationship with the one you love.

Characteristics of Anxiety-Prone People

"I can't even stay 'in the moment' in yoga. Is there such a thing as being yoga challenged?" Lilly joked to her sister after taking her first yoga class. "Ron and I thought it would be a nice thing to do together—especially since my being kind of high strung tends to get us into fights. So when we saw the flyer for this couples yoga class at our gym, we thought it would be the perfect way to learn to relax together.

"Fast-forward to the first class, and there's this really nice yoga teacher talking about 'staying in the moment' and having an 'attitude of gratitude' about being in yoga, and Ron's looking over at me and smiling. But I'm just worrying about everything I have to do today. My house isn't ready for the Christmas party, but I don't have time to clean because I have so much work to finish at the office. And I'm afraid that if I don't finish it, I might get fired. And then, what if I can't get another job? That got me worrying about money. Even with my current income, how am I going to manage getting everyone in my extended family a great holiday gift that's also within my budget? This is such a stressful time of the year!

"Next thing I know, I open my eyes and everyone in the class is on the floor in 'pigeon' or one of those other animal-named yoga positions, and I'm still in 'downward-facing dog' with my butt sticking up in the air! And on top of that, I started to notice this twinge in my lower back, like it was about to spasm. What a mess I am; even yoga stresses me out. Ron was so disappointed when I told him I didn't want to go back."

Lilly's running commentary in her mind, which significantly interfered with her ability to relax and enjoy her yoga class with Ron, is indicative of her *reaction style*: her routine way of responding to the events of everyday life. Reaction styles are like a lens through which you view the world that tints the way you interpret and respond to everyday situations. If you have an *anxiety-prone* reaction style, you often go on "red alert" in response to situations that wouldn't cause others to worry.

To better understand how these anxiety-inducing response patterns relate to the anxiety-prone person, it can be helpful to think of anxiety as occurring on a continuum. Imagine that the left end of the continuum represents little-to-no anxiety, and the right side represents high anxiety that significantly disrupts daily functioning. Optimal levels of anxiety usually fall in the middle range: you don't go through life in a chronic state of alarm, constantly anxious; on the other hand, you don't go through life with anxiety levels so low that you fail to respond to danger or life challenges appropriately. In this middle range, you have appropriate concern about receiving a poor performance review or getting a call from your physician that you need a biopsy to rule out cancer. You want your usual level of anxiety to fall somewhere in the middle range of the continuum. It's like Goldilocks in "The Story of the Three Bears": not too high, not too low, but *just right*. In that middle range, you'd respond to the ups and downs of life with a level of anxiety that was adaptive to the situation at hand. As described earlier, your anxiety levels would match each stressor you encounter.

Lilly, however, experienced a greater degree of reactivity than was optimal. Rather than being "in the moment" during her yoga class, Lilly couldn't stop worrying about the future. This is known as *future focusing*. One of the key components of anxiety is living in the future. Her future-focused worries drove her anxiety level higher than was adaptive given the nonthreatening, relaxing environment of the yoga studio. In fact, her worries even distracted her from what she was doing and left her high and dry, so to speak, while the rest of the class moved from downward-facing dog to other yoga positions.

When Lilly did come back to the present moment to shift her posture and catch up with the class, she noticed a slight twinge in her lower back. This present-focused realization, however, also drove Lilly's anxiety level higher. She interpreted the twinge as a forerunner of serious back problems and began worrying accordingly. This pattern of reaction is known as *maximizing*. Future focusing and maximizing are at the heart of anxiety-prone reaction styles. Let's explore both in more detail.

Future Focusing

If you engage in future focusing, you tend to worry excessively about how upcoming events will pan out. You think of every possible contingency and try to plan accordingly. For example, in order to plan a vacation, you need to be future focused. Yes, it's important to check the weather forecast, think about the activities you will be participating in, and pack with these things in mind. But if you have a future-focused, anxious reaction style, your packing process might be fraught with worry, because you will try to anticipate every possible problem and fret about the fallout if these problems were to occur. Rather than enjoy the anticipation as you envision a relaxing getaway in the Caribbean, you might worry about the possibility of a jellyfish sting or lost luggage. In essence, you spend much of the present looking toward the future with a sense of unease.

Maximizing

If you are a maximizer, you have most likely been accused more than once of making mountains out of molehills. Unlike future focusing, maximizing doesn't cause you to worry about what might go wrong *in the future*. Rather, when you are maximizing, every bump in the road sharply increases your level of anxiety, such as running five minutes late to an appointment because you were stuck in traffic, discovering that the roast you were about to cook for dinner has spoiled, or double booking an appointment with a new client. No one enjoys these everyday mishaps. But if you are a maximizer, they cause your anxiety levels to spike and are accompanied by thoughts that these everyday mishaps have catastrophic implications. You find it much more challenging than non-maximizers do to roll with the punches.

Invasion of the Body Scanners: A Particular Type of Maximizing

A discussion of maximizing wouldn't be complete without mentioning body scanning. Some people who have a maximizing reaction style frequently scan their bodies, remaining on alert for any sign of illness or physical malady. Your partner or your best friend might dismiss a stomachache as a momentary case of indigestion. However, if you are a maximizer with body-scanning tendencies and have a stomachache, you persistently focus on the sensations in your stomach and worry that they are a cause for significant concern. Worries might rush through your mind: *I think I might be coming down with a case of the flu. I hope it's not the H1N1 virus; that would be bad. Maybe it's even worse: it could be the start of colitis or maybe even colon cancer.* Afraid to let the physical sensations in your stomach leave your conscious awareness, you monitor them for any signs that your condition is getting worse.

Unfortunately, this reaction style is insidious. If you are prone to scan your body for indicators of distress, you are likely to notice physical sensations that, for others, would be perceived as insignificant. The physical sensations then spark worry, which increases your levels of tension and anxiety and causes your physical distress to worsen. For example, Lilly's anxiety levels spiked when she noticed the twinge in her lower back during her yoga class. Her mounting anxiety and subsequent increasing muscle tension left her more likely to actually have a back spasm than if she hadn't been distressed by the twinge when she first felt it. It's as if body scanners are trapped in a real-life twist on the classic sci-fi phenomenon, only now it's "Invasion of the Body *Scanners.*"

The Fallout: Rigidity and Irritability

When you're well rested, energized, and calm, you tend to function at your best. You have stores of patience to call on when an unexpected snag arises in your day. You are more likely to remember to be flexible when you make plans or solve problems. But when your levels of anxiety are chronically high, your system is overburdened. Your emotional, mental, and physical energy reserves are depleted, and responding to the demands of life with patience and flexibility becomes more challenging. Rigidity and irritability result.

Imagine that your partner calls to say that he has a deadline at work and has to miss the dinner you had planned together tonight. Or maybe you had scheduled a night out together or were hard at work preparing a romantic dinner at home for just the two of you. Or perhaps you didn't have anything special planned, but your partner's absence means that now you don't have any help with cooking dinner, supervising the kids' homework, and getting them showered and ready for bed.

15

If your internal resources have already been depleted by chronic stress, you are more likely to be derailed by this change in your schedule. You're also more likely to snap at your partner or pick an argument while talking on the phone. Taking a moment to step back and compassionately assess both your disappointment and your partner's work demands may be more conducive to your relationship, but it's not your typical, default reaction. Frequent irritability and rigidity negatively affect your sense of well-being and your interactions with your partner over the long run.

As you can see, you don't need to have an anxiety disorder for anxiety to negatively affect your life. Of course, most people with anxiety disorders do display these anxiety-prone response patterns. For instance, maximizing and future focusing are elements of all the anxiety disorders. But as you'll see in the next section, the anxiety disorders are comprised of specific, unique constellations of *intense* anxiety that can significantly disrupt daily functioning and intimate relationships.

All about Anxiety Disorders

Recognizing and understanding the various anxiety disorders is the first step to healing. The benefit of learning about your specific disorder is that you will discover that you are *not* going crazy and that you are not alone. Finally your symptoms will make sense. It can be freeing and reassuring to have the cause of your suffering identified and to learn that there are effective treatments, that many others have struggled with and *overcome* the same type of fears, and that there are many avenues of help available.

Generalized Anxiety Disorder

If you have *generalized anxiety disorder*, or GAD, worrying may be your main pastime. A barrage of "what ifs" runs through your mind as you go about your day: *What if my doctor finds something wrong at my upcoming annual physical? What if I get lost on the way to my friend's cottage? What if my company begins to downsize due to the bad economy and I lose my job? What if my daughter doesn't get a date for the prom?* The list can go on and on. Pamela, a bank manager, put it this way: "I was at a seminar this morning about diversity in the workplace, and it got me thinking about my GAD. When it comes to worrying, I'm an equal-opportunity employer. I'll worry about anything. I don't discriminate one bit."

This is the hallmark of GAD: the worry doesn't center on a particular *type* of stressor. Rather, as the name of the disorder suggests, the focus of your worry becomes *generalized* to everyday occurrences, and you begin to worry chronically about things that others rarely give a second thought.

When you worry frequently and consistently over long periods of time, an excess of stress hormones, such as cortisol and catecholamines, builds up in your system and can create chronic physical discomfort. People with GAD commonly experience tension headaches, stomachaches and other gastrointestinal upsets, muscle pain, backaches, and exhaustion. While these physical ailments can have many causes, the presence of heightened stress hormones is a major one.

What's more, if you have GAD, you are likely to be more acutely aware of any physical discomfort you experience than would someone without this disorder. Many people with GAD are body scanners, hypersensitive to physical sensations that are even slightly out of the norm. Physical sensations that might slip under the radar for someone without GAD don't go unnoticed by you. And your physical discomforts cause you greater emotional distress than they would someone without GAD, because they increase your anxiety levels.

Thus the physical symptoms of GAD don't just lessen your quality of life. They give you more to worry about, which in turn releases more stress hormones, which in turn may cause the physical discomfort to persist and even intensify. This vicious cycle of worry and heightening physical discomfort can also leave you chronically fatigued. You may find that it's all you can do to find the energy to get through the day. For those with GAD, worry is literally exhausting. What's more, your chronic worry and focus on future catastrophes rob both you and your partner of the pleasures that come from enjoying the present moment.

To recap, GAD consists of the following symptoms:

- Persistent worry about routine, everyday activities, decisions, and events where, unlike with other anxiety disorders, the focus is not on a particular theme

- Chronic physical discomfort, such as gastrointestinal upsets, headaches, or fatigue, that has no other medical explanation; that is, the physical symptoms result from the chronically high levels of stress hormones that are released when you're worrying

Panic Disorder

The three main components of *panic disorder* (PD) are panic attacks, anticipatory anxiety, and avoidance of places or situations that you fear might trigger a panic attack. If you have been diagnosed with PD, you have had at least one panic attack: an episode in which you experienced intense fear accompanied by physical sensations such as a racing heartbeat, shortness of breath, and hot or cold sweats. The physical symptoms occur because your nervous system has revved into fight-or-flight mode. While this state of hyperarousal doesn't pose a serious health threat, people experiencing the physical symptoms of panic attacks typically are afraid they are having a heart attack or some other medical emergency. In the midst of a panic attack, it's also common for people to think they are going "crazy."

Melissa's first panic attack followed the typical pattern. "We were shopping at that new home décor store on a Saturday afternoon. One minute I was fine, looking at new bedspreads, and the next thing I knew, my heart was racing and I couldn't catch my breath. I was desperate to get out of there, but was so flustered that I couldn't figure out where the exit was. I felt like I was going insane. Thank goodness my husband was there; I don't know what I would have done without him. He took my hand, led me out of the store, got the car, and took me to the ER. I thought for sure I was having a heart attack. By the time we got to the hospital, though, the pain, fear, shortness of breath—everything was gone. The only remnants of the attack were my frayed nerves and embarrassing sweat stains on the underarms of my blouse.

"The doctors checked me over, gave me an EKG to check my heart, and ended up telling me it was 'just nerves.' *Just* nerves! It was as if they were telling me that the absolutely horrific experience I had just had was in my imagination. That couldn't be further from the case."

If the experience Melissa described hits home for you, you are among millions of people who have had a panic attack. But having had a panic attack—or even many panic attacks—doesn't necessarily mean that you have panic disorder. The disorder develops when you begin spending lots of time worrying about if, when, and where another panic attack will occur. This is called *anticipatory anxiety*. If you have panic disorder, you play out possible scenarios of your next attack in your mind. Next you begin avoiding the places where you think another attack is likely to occur. This is the third and final component of PD: avoidance.

> Melissa's description of the development of her panic disorder captures the experience of anticipatory anxiety and avoidance: "No matter what I do, I still can't get that first panic attack out of my mind. Just the thought of being back in that store gets me shaking. A few weeks later, I had another attack while I was grocery shopping. It was the same as the first time, except this time my husband wasn't there to help me. And despite the doctor's earlier reassurance, I was again sure that my heart was giving out and I would die.

"Now I feel at the mercy of my panic attacks. I never know when one is going to just pop up out of the blue. I can't prevent them, and I can't stop them once they start. So I try to avoid going into big retail stores. That's where my attacks seem to occur. If I really *have* to go, I try to get in and out as fast as possible. It's the only thing I can do to get a handle on my panic attacks."

Some people with PD become so afraid of having a panic attack in a public place that they rarely venture from their homes. This is known as panic disorder with *agoraphobia*: an intense fear of being in public places. Whether or not you have agoraphobia, the anticipatory anxiety about panic attacks and the resulting avoidance distinguish people with PD from those who have an occasional panic attack.

To recap, the three main components of panic disorder are as follows:

- One or more panic attacks

- Anticipatory anxiety: frequent worry about when and where the next panic attack might take place

- Avoidance of the places and situations that you fear might spark another panic attack

In response to your anticipatory anxiety and avoidance, your partner may begin taking on tasks that you no longer can do. For example, Melissa's husband began doing all of the grocery shopping. While sharing tasks is part of well-functioning relationships, this division of labor takes a negative twist when it is dictated by one partner's anxiety. (We discuss this concept further in chapters 7 and 8.) Panic disorder can affect intimate relationships in other ways as well. Melissa's avoidance limited the activities she and her husband could do together. Before her PD set in, they had enjoyed spending Saturday afternoons working on home-improvement projects. Now trips to home-improvement stores together were out of the question.

Specific Phobias

Specific phobias (SP) are an extreme fear of and aversion to a particular thing or situation. Some common specific phobias are fears of dogs, snakes, spiders, heights, the sight of blood, and needles. If you have an SP, the terror you experience when you are exposed to the object or situation you fear (the *phobic stimulus*) defies reason. Reason with yourself as you might, your extreme fear does not subside.

The result of SP is that you are likely to go out of your way to avoid your phobic stimulus. If you fear spiders, you probably avoid cleaning out cobwebby basements. Or you limit the types of vacations or leisure activities you plan with your partner to avoid any places where encounters with spiders are likely. If you fear heights, it's unlikely that you would choose to live on the top floor of a high-rise. You and your partner's choice of residence might be limited and, in a sense, dictated by your fear.

Unlike people with panic disorder, you probably don't spend much time worrying about your phobic stimulus. Unless you are confronted with it, your phobia most likely won't even cross your mind on any given day. Thus, specific phobias generally do not affect people's lives as pervasively as do the other anxiety disorders. They can, however, have a considerable impact on a relationship. It's one thing for you to curtail your life to avoid your phobia; it's another to curtail your partner's life as well.

While there are too many phobias to list exhaustively, common categories of phobias include the following.

Situational. Fears in this category are related to the man-made world. Common situational phobias are driving on highways, driving or walking over bridges or through tunnels, being in enclosed spaces such as elevators, flying, and taking public transportation.

Natural environment. These fears involve situations encountered in nature (but do not include fears of animals or insects). The most common phobias in this category are fears of storms, water, and heights.

Animal. These phobias involve the intense fear of a particular creature in the animal kingdom. Fears of snakes, spiders, and other insects are common types of animal phobias. Anxiety-disorders expert David Barlow (2002) notes that many of these phobias have a genetic or evolutionary component.

Blood, injection, or injury. This category consists of three specific phobias. Blood phobia involves an intense fear of the sight of blood or bleeding; injection phobia, a fear of needles, including receiving or even witnessing injections; and injury phobia, an extreme fear of sustaining or seeing physical injuries. Blood, injection, or injury is the most common category of phobias. It is also the only category of phobias in which exposure to the feared situation can bring about a drop in blood pressure that can lead to fainting. (In the other phobias and anxiety disorders in general, fear usually triggers an increase in blood pressure.) Again, researchers think that there is a genetic component to this phobia for people who do experience a drop in blood pressure (ibid.).

Social Anxiety Disorder

If you have *social anxiety disorder* (SAD), you most likely have an intense fear of being seen, criticized, or judged by others. For some people this fear only occurs in specific situations, such as public speaking or other types of performing, and is known as *specific* SAD. For others, however, the fear applies across a broader range of social contexts. When this is the case, *generalized* SAD is diagnosed.

The fear associated with generalized SAD may lead you to limit your social activities considerably and to significantly curtail your professional or academic life. You might be afraid to go to parties, participate in class, or attend staff meetings. You might feel dread for days or weeks in anticipation of the situations or events you fear, or you might even avoid them entirely. Your social anxiety might dictate your career choice or your decision to pursue or forego higher education. In some cases, people with severe generalized SAD are afraid of answering the phone, eating or writing in front of others, or using public restrooms.

After months of avoiding going out to dinner with friends and family, Jim finally admitted to his girlfriend, Amy, that he felt extremely uncomfortable in social situations. Particularly, he had trouble tolerating larger social gatherings in which he was expected to interact with others. Jim had even earned his undergraduate and master's degrees online for that very reason.

"It's not that I don't like people," Jim told Amy. "I love spending time with you, and I'm okay with my family or some of my closest friends. But when I'm around a lot of your friends or my colleagues, I can't stand it. My face gets all red, I start to sweat, and I'm mortified that everyone can see how anxious I am. I know they notice, so I usually make sure to leave as quickly as possible or avoid going in the first place. Whenever I have to go to an event, like your cousin's wedding, I spend most of the time in the restroom anyway. It's the only space where I can have some privacy and calm down. I don't want you to think that I don't like your family or your friends. It's just that, unless an event is absolutely mandatory, it's better if I don't go."

Physical symptoms associated with social anxiety disorder include heart palpitations, faintness, blushing, and profuse sweating when you are confronted with your feared social situations. Unfortunately, the physical distress related to the fear creates yet another reason to avoid social situations: worry that others will notice the signs of your physical distress and judge you negatively. The fear of feeling judged and scrutinized by others can also make people with generalized SAD reluctant to pursue counseling to address the disorder.

To recap, SAD is characterized by the following symptoms:

- Intense fear of being seen and judged by others

- Physical symptoms: racing heart, feeling faint or dizzy (but not actually fainting), feeling hot or flushed, breaking out in a sweat that is caused by neither the room temperature nor physical exertion

- Avoidance of social settings in which you might feel judged or under scrutiny

- One of two presentations: specific, occurring only in response to specific social situations such as public speaking, or generalized, occurring in a broader range of social contexts

Obsessive-Compulsive Disorder

During the past decade, *obsessive-compulsive disorder* (OCD) has rocketed into mainstream awareness as characters with OCD have appeared in popular movies and TV shows. OCD has likewise been discussed and even showcased on reality television. You may have become familiar with characters who are so afraid of being contaminated by germs that they wash their hands compulsively, wear gloves in public year-round, or carry hand sanitizer everywhere. Or you might have seen a character who engages in a repetitive counting ritual such as locking and unlocking a door a set number of times (think of Jack Nicholson's character in *As Good as It Gets*). All of these behaviors fall into the category of OCD.

If you have OCD, you experience persistent, recurring thoughts (*obsessions*) that center on a given theme, such as fear of germ contamination. To quell these fears, you usually develop a ritual or routine (*compulsion*) that calms the anxiety spurred by the obsessive thought. Compulsive rituals can include repeating phrases or tasks, hoarding items, or compulsively arranging objects so that they are perfectly symmetrical or aligned. For example, Emma entered therapy after she learned that her coworkers called her the "broken record," because she often repeated the last three or four words of her sentences in an effort, as she said, "to say it just right." After learning about the nickname, Emma tried to curtail her habit but was unsuccessful. "I can't calm down until I get the words right," she told her therapist. "The second I get it right, my whole body relaxes, and if I don't let myself keep trying until I get it, I can't get anything else done."

Robert developed a different form of OCD. He decided to enter therapy because he couldn't bring himself to throw anything away. His boyfriend had begged him multiple times to throw out the stacks of mail, newspapers, bills, and receipts that covered their floors and furniture. Robert said he'd try, but he never succeeded. He just kept adding to the piles. Finally his boyfriend gave up and left him.

"He said he couldn't live with someone who refused to keep the place in some semblance of order," Robert told his therapist. "I wish he could understand that I *need* to have my papers exactly as they are; that *is* a semblance of order—for me. I can't have it any other way. But I also don't want to spend the rest of my life alone."

Whether you're a hoarder, like Robert, or have another particular obsession and compulsive response behavior, if you have OCD you feel that you *must* engage in your particular ritual when your obsessive thoughts occur. Or your ritual may involve avoiding situations or objects that provoke obsessions.

The following is a summary of OCD obsessions and compulsions.

Obsessions. These are persistent, intrusive thoughts centering on one or two themes, such as fear of contamination or fear of an impending catastrophe.

Compulsions. These are rituals that ease the anxiety caused by an obsessive thought; however, a small percentage of people with OCD experience the intrusive, obsessive thoughts without engaging in any particular ritual. Common compulsions are:

- *Ordering:* Arranging objects in your home, workplace, or vehicle, or on your computer desktop in a particular configuration.

- *Checking:* Repeatedly checking various objects in order to feel safe—for example, compulsively checking to make sure the stove is turned off, the doors are locked, or the cabinets are closed. Often this includes switching an appliance on and off a set number of times, unlocking and locking the door, or opening and closing doors repeatedly.

- *Sanitizing:* Engaging in rituals to either eliminate the presence of germs or avoid contact with them—for instance, frequently applying hand sanitizer or wearing gloves to minimize the amount of germs that come in contact with your hands.

- *Repeating:* Saying phrases or taking actions repeatedly, or until you feel it's just "right," such as reading the same passage over and over, or rewriting an e-mail repeatedly.

- *Hoarding:* An inability to discard items in your home or office, such as mail, magazines, or receipts, out of fear that you might need them in the future. This also includes purchasing large quantities of similar items. The collection of possessions often becomes so extensive that stacks of belongings cover furniture and a significant portion of floor space.

Post-Traumatic Stress Disorder

Unlike the other anxiety disorders, which don't necessarily develop in response to a particular event or situation, *post-traumatic stress disorder* (PTSD) develops in response to a trauma. A trauma is any situation in which you experience intense fear or helplessness in response to the perception that you or someone you care about is in significant danger. Typical examples of traumas are being the victim of a violent crime such as robbery or rape, experiencing childhood incest, being in a car accident or natural disaster, and being in a war either as a soldier or as a civilian bystander. Less commonly recognized traumas include witnessing crimes, accidents, or natural disasters and learning of a loved one's death or victimization.

As you can see, a wide variety of traumatic incidents can precipitate PTSD. However, experiencing a trauma doesn't necessarily mean that you will develop PTSD. This is because the experience of trauma is subjective. No two people experience the same event in the same way. For example, people who were in Manhattan on September 11, 2001, when the Twin Towers were attacked, experienced the same event. However, not everyone developed PTSD. Likewise, of those who watched media coverage of the event or lost a loved one there, only some developed PTSD.

Although we don't know why some people develop PTSD, we do know that the symptoms can be debilitating. This was the case for Larry, a forty-three-year-old tax attorney who, a year later, was still struggling every day with the aftermath of a car accident.

"Car accidents happen every day, and people brush themselves off and go on with their lives," Larry told his therapist. "I don't understand why I can't. My collarbone was broken on impact, but it healed over six months ago. The rest of me seems to be getting worse though, not better. I used to enjoy my commute to work in the mornings. I would listen to the radio, drink my coffee, and enjoy my last few minutes to myself before the workday got underway.

"Now I endure my morning drive. Almost every time I pass through an intersection, I tense up. If I even see the slightest shadow of another car in my peripheral vision, I get startled. And when I try to listen to the radio, my heart starts pounding, so now I drive in silence. And I can't, for the life of me, make myself drive through the intersection where I was hit, so I have to go four blocks out of my way to avoid it."

The avoidance of anything reminiscent of the original trauma—the intersection where Larry was hit, the radio program he was listening to—is a hallmark of PTSD. *Hypervigilance*, as demonstrated by Larry's exaggerated startle response when driving and his tension while he was on the road, is another hallmark. Trouble focusing, disrupted sleep, emotional numbness, and *flashbacks* (intrusive memories of the traumatic event) are other components of PTSD. They were all evident as Larry continued his story:

"I've been slipping at work, too," Larry said quietly, looking down at the floor. "I keep making careless mistakes. It's as if my head's not quite in the game. I think it's partly because I'm not getting much sleep. I awaken startled at least three or four times a night, and when I do finally get to sleep and stay asleep, I dream over and over again of the car crashing. My doctor says that my collarbone's completely healed, but I keep getting these pains in my shoulder near where my car door smashed into it. My wife says that she misses my laughter, that I don't seem like the same person anymore. She's right: I'm not the same person I was before the accident."

As Larry's case demonstrates, the effects of a trauma for people with PTSD can reverberate in the mind and body for months and years to come. Partners of people with PTSD often feel helpless in the face of their loved ones' suffering; indeed, in many ways, they are. While partners can offer compassion and care in an effort to support your healing process, they cannot mend the symptoms of PTSD. Partners feel powerless and resentful toward the trauma and its impact on you and your relationship, and they feel guilty that they are unable to help. As Larry and his wife discovered, with PTSD time doesn't heal *all* wounds.

Here's a recap of the signs and symptoms associated with PTSD:

- Avoidance of things associated with the traumatic event (places, sights, sounds, smells, people, situations, and so on).

- Hypervigilance, where the body remains in a state of chronic high alert. This often results in an exaggerated startle response, always being tense or on edge, and disrupted sleep cycles.

- Difficulty concentrating.

- Emotional numbness.

- Flashbacks, which are intrusive memories of, or nightmares about, the traumatic event. They can take the form of images or "movies" of the event that flash into awareness. They can also manifest as physical sensations that occurred during the event. These are known as *body memories*. Larry's shoulder pain was a body memory.

Now that you're familiar with the various ways that anxiety can present itself, the following exercises can help you get a better idea of the ways that anxiety affects you. The self-knowledge you will gain from completing the exercises will prepare you for the next steps in your healing process.

Self-Assessment Exercises

The following two questionnaires will help you understand the degree to which anxiety affects your life and relationship. Exercise 1.1, "The Anxiety Self-Assessment Tool," focuses on how anxiety is affecting your own life. Exercise 1.2, "Assessing the Impact of Anxiety on Your Relationship," focuses on how your stress or anxiety reactions affect your spouse or partner.

Neither of these questionnaires is intended to be used as a diagnostic tool. Rather, they are best seen as general indicators of anxiety, and they will provide you with a sense of your own level of distress and the degree to which your distress or anxiety affects your spouse or partner. You can also use these tests to help you decide whether it would be a good idea to see a mental health professional, who could more precisely diagnose your condition and provide effective treatment options.

EXERCISE 1.1
The Anxiety Self-Assessment Tool

This self-assessment allows you to rate how frequently you experience anxiety and stress reactions. For each statement, pick the response that feels most true for you. It's important to refrain from self-judgment as you consider the statements; simply let your responses reflect how you honestly feel the majority of the time. Note that the multiple-choice options are not the same for all statements, so you'll want to read the potential responses carefully.

1. I feel tense or jittery.

    a. Rarely or never

    b. Sometimes

    c. Often

    d. Very often

2. I anticipate and worry about what can go wrong in the future.

    a. Rarely or never

    b. Sometimes

    c. Often

    d. Very often

3. I am easygoing.

    a. Very often

    b. Often

    c. Sometimes

    d. Rarely or never

4. In the mornings, I wake up worried.

    a. Rarely or never

    b. Sometimes

    c. Often

    d. Very often

5. I go out of my way to avoid the situations or places that cause me worry.

    a. Rarely or never

    b. Sometimes

    c. Often

    d. Very often

6. When I go to bed at night, I easily fall asleep *and* am able to sleep throughout the night.

    a. Very often

    b. Often

    c. Sometimes

    d. Rarely or never

7. I experience sudden waves of panic that seem to pop up out of the blue.

    a. Rarely or never

    b. Sometimes

    c. Often

    d. Very often

8. I feel relaxed or at ease.
   a. Very often
   b. Often
   c. Sometimes
   d. Rarely or never

9. I feel as if something catastrophic is about to happen.
   a. Rarely or never
   b. Sometimes
   c. Often
   d. Very often

10. I experience unexplained, intense stomach upsets, head-aches, or various muscle aches and pains.
    a. Rarely or never
    b. Sometimes
    c. Often
    d. Very often

11. I've had a panic attack, and I worry about when and where the next one will occur.
    a. Rarely or never
    b. Sometimes
    c. Often
    d. Very often

12. I have an intense fear of a particular object or situation (such as spiders, heights, or the sight of blood) and go out my way to avoid coming into contact with this object or situation.
    a. Rarely or never
    b. Sometimes
    c. Often
    d. Very often

13. I worry about being judged by others, and I try to avoid situations in which I fear this will occur.

    a. Rarely or never

    b. Sometimes

    c. Often

    d. Very often

14. I have persistent, intrusive thoughts centered on one or several themes (such as a fear of germ contamination or a fear that something is out of order).

    a. Rarely or never

    b. Sometimes

    c. Often

    d. Very often

15. I experience persistent, intrusive memories of past traumas.

    a. Rarely or never

    b. Sometimes

    c. Often

    d. Very often

Scoring Your Self-Assessment

Again, note that the order of the responses differs for some statements. For statements 1 through 6, if you circled "c" or "d" once or more, and for statements 7 through 15, if you circled "b," "c," or "d" at least once, then it's highly likely that anxiety is significantly affecting your life. The time-out method presented in the next chapter will help you better *regulate*, or manage, your anxiety. With this method, you can learn to control your anxiety, rather than allowing it to control you.

If you circled "a" or "b" for statements 1 through 6 and "a" for statements 7 through 15, then anxiety has affected you but not significantly. The time-out method in chapter 2 can be of great benefit to you. Regardless of your levels of anxiety, the abilities to recognize your levels of arousal and to regulate your emotions accordingly, both of which you will gain through the time-out method, will be an asset in both your personal and your professional life. Even if your self-assessment scores indicate that you don't experience high levels of anxiety on a daily basis, you might choose to use daily time-outs whenever you do experience anger or irritability. Doing so can not only promote relaxation, but also enhance your communication with your partner and improve your relationship. Likewise, the tools presented in chapter 3 for creating and sustaining a daily relaxation routine can also significantly enhance your ability to engage in the present moment with a sense of calm and ease.

EXERCISE 1.2
Assessing the Impact of
Anxiety on Your Relationship

This assessment focuses on the interactions between you and your partner so that you can evaluate how a particular interaction affects your sense of connection. For each statement, pick the response that feels most true for you. It's important to refrain from self-judgment as you consider these statements; simply let your responses reflect how you honestly feel about your relationship.

1. My partner proposes logic-based solutions when I express fear or worry.

    a. Rarely or never

    b. Sometimes

    c. Often

    d. Very often

2. I feel that my partner doesn't "get" what I'm going through.

    a. Rarely or never

    b. Sometimes

    c. Often

    d. Very often

3. I end up feeling frustrated, unheard, or misunderstood when I go to my partner for support about my anxiety.

    a. Rarely or never

    b. Sometimes

    c. Often

    d. Very often

4. I feel that my partner isn't there for me when I most need him or her.

    a. Rarely or never

    b. Sometimes

    c. Often

    d. Very often

5. When I'm upset and anxious, my partner seems angry or frustrated with me.

    a. Rarely or never

    b. Sometimes

    c. Often

    d. Very often

6. When I'm worried, stressed, or fearful, my partner gets stressed and nervous as well.

   a. Rarely or never

   b. Sometimes

   c. Often

   d. Very often

7. It seems as if my partner withdraws from me when I'm upset.

   a. Rarely or never

   b. Sometimes

   c. Often

   d. Very often

8. I feel fearful or uncomfortable participating in an activity that is important to my partner.

   a. Rarely or never

   b. Sometimes

   c. Often

   d. Very often

9. I feel that my partner criticizes me for not being more rational or sensible.

   a. Rarely or never

   b. Sometimes

   c. Often

   d. Very often

10. I feel that my partner judges me as being inflexible, stubborn, and unwilling to face my fears.

    a. Rarely or never

    b. Sometimes

c. Often

d. Very often

11. I criticize my partner for not being empathic enough.

a. Rarely or never

b. Sometimes

c. Often

d. Very often

12. I resent my partner for his or her inability to understand me.

a. Rarely or never

b. Sometimes

c. Often

d. Very often

13. I resent my partner for his or her inability to respond appropriately to my needs.

a. Rarely or never

b. Sometimes

c. Often

d. Very often

14. I think my partner resents me for frequently expressing my concerns, fears, and worries.

a. Rarely or never

b. Sometimes

c. Often

d. Very often

15. I think that my partner is overprotective of me because of my anxiety.

a. Rarely or never

b. Sometimes

c. Often

d. Very often

16. I think that my partner takes on more than his or her share of responsibilities to protect me from the things that heighten my anxiety.

a. Rarely or never

b. Sometimes

c. Often

d. Very often

17. I worry that I'm too dependent on my partner.

a. Rarely or never

b. Sometimes

c. Often

d. Very often

18. I worry that I am overburdening my partner.

a. Rarely or never

b. Sometimes

c. Often

d. Very often

Scoring Your Assessment

If you circled "c" or "d" on at least two questions, it's very likely that your anxiety is significantly affecting your relationship. Occasional communication hiccups, misunderstandings, anger, and rifts in your sense of connection are inevitable in any relationship. However, when heightened anxiety enters the picture, these bumps in the road occur with more frequency, tensions build, and your sense of connection and partnership—the basis of your relationship—is thrown off balance. The remaining chapters in part 1 will help you get your anxiety levels more under control to lessen their impact on the quality of your connection with your partner. In the final two parts of the book, you will gain knowledge and skills that will enable you to establish new ways of communicating and interacting with your partner. You can gain a stronger sense of connection and companionship.

If you circled only "a's" and "b's," your anxiety levels haven't significantly affected the quality of your interactions with your partner. That being said, there's always room for growth in a relationship. The anxiety-reduction techniques and communication practices that are taught in the remainder of this book will provide you with invaluable skills that can serve to enhance your experience of connection and contentment in your relationship.

Wrapping It Up

For all readers of this book, the material that follows will enhance your ability to regulate your emotions, enrich your communication, and transform your experience of intimacy. These are the powerful building blocks of a successful relationship. This process begins, however, by developing a solid relationship with yourself. As you learn and implement the anxiety-reduction tools in the next two chapters, you will find that you are able to provide yourself with the sense of well-being and empowerment that your anxiety has taken from you. The freedom you discover when you take responsibility for yourself will lead to an ever-evolving and expanding connection with yourself and your partner. With knowledge regarding your anxiety and its impact on your relationship under your belt, it's now time to get into action.

chapter 2

Recognizing Your Anxiety Triggers and Plugging the Dam

Now that you've identified the ways in which anxiety manifests in your life and affects your intimate relationship, you are better equipped to combat your anxiety when it arises. It's been said that knowledge is power. However, knowledge without action is insufficient to break ingrained, habitual responses. This is because, as neuroscientist Joseph LeDoux (1996) notes, the brain is wired so that it's far easier for us to become flooded with emotion than to manage that emotion with reason. If the emotion-based and logic-based structures of your brain were having a shouting match, the emotion-based structures would win. It's as if the emotion-based structures come equipped with a megaphone, while the logic-based structures only have a dime-store microphone to convey the voice of reason. The unfortunate result is that the voice of emotion comes across strongly, loudly, and clearly, while the voice of reason is present but muted in the background.

That's why, when anxiety strikes, it's easy to become overwhelmed by a flood of fearful emotions—emotions that knowledge and reason alone are insufficient to combat. It is imperative that you have an arsenal of tools that can quickly level the playing field, calming your anxiety enough to enable you to respond to your stress from a more balanced place of reason and logic. Psychotherapists call this skill *self-regulation*. To make the goal of self-regulation a reality, this chapter teaches the time-out method, a strategy to stop your anxiety in its tracks when you become triggered and to prevent your anxiety from triggering tension and conflict between you and your partner. This practice provides the foundation for all the other tools and techniques in this book. We cannot overemphasize the importance of taking time-outs.

Time-Out for Adults: Laying the Groundwork

Taking a time-out involves three steps: (1) recognizing when you're triggered, (2) initiating the time-out, and (3) enacting self-soothing techniques. You may associate the term "time-out" with a disciplinary technique used to respond to small children who are overwhelmed or frustrated or have lost control. Although a time-out benefits a child, the child rarely welcomes it. In contrast, you will discover that your time-out is a gift that you give yourself and your partner. Far from punishment, the time-out provides a way to remove yourself from a triggering situation and gain control of your reactions. In addition to being an effective way to manage your own anxiety, it also helps your relationship. Connection and effective communication are impeded by habitual, knee-jerk responses to frustration, perceived threats, and life pressures. The time-out method enables you to put anxiety-fueled interactions with your partner on hold until you defuse your anxiety and gain perspective.

Once your anxiety has diminished, you can resume interactions with greater equilibrium.

Before the Storm: Recognizing When You're Triggered

Just as every flood begins with the gathering of storm clouds, every anxiety reaction begins with mounting tension and fear. Until you are aware of the signs of increasing anxiety, it can seem as if your anxiety just pops up out of the blue. For many, especially people with anxiety disorders such as panic disorder and PTSD, it often seems as if anxiety levels can reach flood stage in mere seconds without warning. However, with a little knowledge, attention, and practice, you can learn to recognize the gathering storm clouds and take preventive measures.

How do you anticipate the coming storm? You begin by identifying your red flags: indicators that your anxiety levels are on the rise and that you are becoming triggered. Triggers typically take the form of thoughts and ideas (*cognitions*), emotions, and physical sensations, all of which are described next. Understanding them will help you identify your own constellation of anxiety indicators.

Cognitive Indicators

A stream of running commentary accompanies each of us in our mind as we go through the day, regardless of whether we are anxious. It provides back-chatter as we run errands, complete work activities, or engage in conversations with our partners and friends. For example, as we shop in the grocery store, we internally deliberate over which apples to pick out, which brand of crackers to buy, or which checkout line to enter: *Hmm, this apple is bruised; I think I'll put it back. Russ didn't like that brand of crackers the last time I bought them, so I'll try this kind and see if he likes it. I'm really not in the mood to stand in a long line today; I think I'll do the self-checkout since that usually goes faster—wow, look who's on the cover of that magazine...*

If you pay attention, this running commentary can tip you off when your anxiety levels are on the rise. Watch out for common thoughts that accompany escalating anxiety:

- *I can't bear this.*

- *I can't stand this.*

- *I'm going crazy.*

- *This is going to be a disaster.*

- *I can't face this.*

- *This is too much to handle.*

- *I can't get it all done.*

- *I'm losing control.*

- *I feel helpless.*

- *Why doesn't my partner understand?*

- *Why doesn't my partner know what I need?*

Emotional Indicators

Emotions are feeling-rich experiences that can powerfully shape our experience of each moment. While nervousness and panic are obvious emotional correlates of anxiety, there are many emotional indicators of rising anxiety. Keep an open mind as you read the following list, and with each emotion, take a moment to recall an occasion when you experienced it. Allow a hint of the feeling to gently surface, and see if you commonly associate it with your experience of anxiety.

Anger	Impatience	Resentment
Despair	Inadequacy	Sadness
Exhaustion	Irritability	Shame
Failure	Nervousness	Terror
Fear	Overwhelm	
Frustration	Panic	

Physical Indicators

The physical indicators of anxiety result from the activation of the sympathetic nervous system and sometimes also the parasympathetic nervous system. You can think of the *sympathetic nervous system* as the gas pedal of your nervous system, revving up your engine so that you can defend yourself. When confronted with a frightening stimulus that the body perceives as a threat, the sympathetic nervous system revs the body into fight-or-flight mode. Your heartbeat increases and the blood flow to your extremities decreases and is diverted into the organs and muscles that mobilize you to either defend yourself or flee. In fact, most of the uncomfortable and even disconcerting physical components of anxiety result from the sympathetic nervous system kicking into action to protect you from any physical danger. Or, in some cases, the sympathetic nervous system *and* parasympathetic nervous system rev concurrently (which begins the freeze response, a third possible reaction to an anxiety-causing situation). This concurrent revving can spark sensations such as light-headedness or muscle weakness (listed shortly) and is especially common for people who have PTSD.

Ideally, following sympathetic nervous system activation, the parasympathetic nervous system kicks in to quiet the revving of the sympathetic nervous system, calming the body and defusing the anxiety response. The *parasympathetic nervous system* can be thought of as the brakes of your autonomic nervous system. To effectively manage your anxiety, a well-functioning interplay of parasympathetic and sympathetic arousal needs to take place in the autonomic nervous system. The time-out techniques introduced in the following exercises will help you engage your parasympathetic nervous system and put the brakes on your escalating anxiety. In other words, as you learn to better manage your anxiety with the tools in this book, you will teach your body to nudge the parasympathetic nervous system into action to lessen the revving of the sympathetic nervous system.

Knowing the physical markers of your stress response is the first line of defense in preventing further escalation of your anxiety. The following is a list of common physical indicators of autonomic nervous system activation:

- Light-headedness

- Dizziness

- A sensation of shakiness

- Racing heartbeat

- Nausea

- Stomach pains or cramping

- Stomach upsets

- Hot flashes

- Cold sweats

- Tingling in hands or feet

- Cold, clammy hands or feet

- Muscle weakness

- Muscle tension or tightness in arms, legs, chest, or shoulders

EXERCISE 2.1
Recognize When You're Triggered

In this exercise you will recall a *recent* experience of heightened anxiety to help you identify your unique constellation of cognitive, emotional, and physical indicators. For this exercise you need to set aside ten or fifteen minutes and find a quiet space where you won't be disturbed. Review the cognitive, emotional, and physical indicators of overreactions listed previously to help you more readily identify your own indicators of anxiety as they crop up during the exercise. You can also keep the book handy, opened to this section, so that you can peruse the list of indicators again after you've completed the exercise. You'll want to have pen and paper ready as well, so you can jot down your identified triggers at the end of the exercise. Getting them down on paper while the experience is fresh in your mind is a helpful memory aid—and creates a list of your triggers that you can refer back to.

The triggers you are beginning to identify can feel like knee-jerk reactions; some of them, such as muscle tension, might even have been occurring under the radar of your awareness. As you're learning to identify your warning signs of an overreaction, it can be helpful to keep your list of your triggers handy. We suggest keeping this list in your purse or wallet so that you can pull it out, scan your triggers, and take a quick inventory when you notice that you feel anxious or tense. When you notice you are experiencing any of the triggers on your list, it's time for a time-out.

There are several ways to do this exercise. You can read through the script a few times to familiarize yourself with it and then follow it from memory, you can record the script and listen to it while doing the exercise, or you can ask a friend or a therapist to read the script to you while you follow the instructions. Simply choose the method that works best for you. Once you have prepared, you're ready to begin.

Call to mind a time when you were feeling very anxious.
Reach back in your memory and remember a time when

you felt overcome by fear or worry—and when that fear or worry felt uncomfortable, distressing, or unsettling. And once you have recalled a recent occasion when you felt very anxious, for a moment or two let yourself reexperience the thoughts and feelings you had then. What were the sensations in your hands, in the skin on your face? What did you sense in your shoulders, your torso, your legs, your feet? What thoughts were running through your mind? What did you say to yourself? What emotions did you feel? Were there other people with you, or were you alone? Were you indoors or outside? Were you in a noisy public setting—or in the quiet of your home?

Just sit with the memory of these feelings, these thoughts, and these physical sensations. And as you sit with this memory, allow the feelings, thoughts, and sensations to arise fresh so that you experience them now, in the present. Begin to sense them—just letting the feelings come up, becoming more intense—all the while knowing that you are sitting safely in the present and that you can heighten or lessen these sensations and feelings as you choose; you are in control.

And as you invite these sensations to become stronger and stronger, know that these familiar, uncomfortable feelings and sensations are present in this moment to help you—reexperiencing them now, in the safety of your quiet room, can help you learn to better identify them and quell them in the future.

Can you identify what you were thinking during that situation in the past? As you reexperience the anxiety, what words or phrases come up for you? And what feelings come up with those thoughts? Can you identify the feelings or emotions that accompanied the experience? Take your time to acknowledge and label each emotion that you sense.

And now move your attention to your body. It's said that the body is the file cabinet for the mind. Where in your body do you feel tension, discomfort, "dis-ease"? In your stomach, your jaw, your shoulders, your eyes?

And now that you have identified the thoughts, the feelings, and the physical sensations that go along with your experience of anxiety, turn down the dial that controls the intensity of your sensations...lowering it smoothly, bit by bit, allowing sensations of calm, of ease, of relaxation to flow from the center of your chest all the way down to your fingertips and toes and up to the top of your head, as you return fully to the present moment—where your feet remain firmly anchored on the ground. And as you come back fully to the present, allow yourself to feel good as you acknowledge that you have returned from this brief journey into the past with new knowledge that will help you combat your worry and anxiety in the future.

Finding a Port in the Storm: Initiating a Time-Out

Once you're able to recognize the cognitive, emotional, and physical indicators of your anxiety responses, you can deal with your anxiety before it escalates. No longer at the mercy of your anxiety, you now can take control through a time-out, defusing your anxiety and the potential conflict with your partner. To maximize the effectiveness of your time-out, preparation is key so that in the heat of the moment, you can focus completely on de-escalating your anxiety. To prepare, you will need to decide on a physical space for your at-home time-outs, convey to your partner your plan to take time-outs as needed, and establish a time-out procedure that you both will follow.

Deciding on a Physical Space

Whether you're at home, at work, or out in a public place, it's important to have a set location where you can take a time-out as needed. It's often easiest to establish a time-out space at home, since you generally have the most control over your surroundings there and the greatest chance of ensuring privacy. Many people choose the bedroom, a guest room, or a small home office. We advise, if possible, against choosing a common area that your partner or your children might need to access while you're engaged in your time-out. If you live in a mild climate, you might consider making your time-out space an outside patio or your backyard, as long as it is tranquil, comfortable, private, and accessible day and night.

After choosing a location, you can take some additional steps to create a soothing, relaxing environment. Some people like soft, low lighting, perhaps with candles. You may want soothing music in the background. Make sure to unplug or silence any phones so that you won't be interrupted. Anyone who calls can wait the extra ten or fifteen minutes while you regain a sense of calm. You might want to hang a "Do Not Disturb" sign on the door. In creating your time-out space thoughtfully, you're honoring yourself and your commitment to recovery from high anxiety.

When you're out in public or at a friend's house and need a few minutes of privacy for a time-out, restrooms offer you a location where privacy is ensured. They are usually available no matter where you are and are relatively easy to find. Excusing yourself to go to the restroom is also a quick, socially acceptable way to engage in a time-out that never requires an explanation for your temporary exit. Whether you are with your partner, with others, or alone when the need to take a time-out in a public place arises, excusing yourself to go to the restroom will give you the time and space you need.

Of course, there will be times when you simply can't get privacy. If you are a passenger in a car or bus, for example, we suggest that you tell your partner that you need a few minutes to yourself to take a time-out. Or, if there are other occupants of the vehicle who are unaware of your time-out procedure, you can simply ask to take a moment to yourself to relax. Any of the relaxation techniques you will perform during a time-out can be performed as you sit quietly in your seat.

If you are the driver and are with your partner or others, you might simply state that you'd like to listen to the radio or a CD rather than converse for the remainder of the ride. Since you can't engage in the relaxation techniques while you are driving, it's important to refrain from interaction that might intensify your anxiety or fuel conflict during this time. Since people commonly listen to music without talking when in a car, this is a socially acceptable way for you to give yourself some mental space without having to notify others of your time-out procedure. If your partner is in the car with you, you can say that you need a time-out and will take one as soon as you get to where you are going. In the interim, you can request that the two of you listen to soothing music (see the resources in appendix D for a recommended CD of ambient music). When you arrive at your destination, you can take the time and space you need to engage in your time-out.

When your partner is still close by, the success of your time-outs depends, in large part, on your partner's respect for and understanding of what you're doing. This hinges on how well you have explained, in advance, the nature and purpose of your time-outs. The development of a mutual understanding regarding your time-outs is fundamental, whether or not you take your time-outs in close proximity to your partner.

Explaining Time-Outs to Your Partner

A time-out provides you with a much-needed opportunity to stop your mounting anxiety in its tracks. It also serves as a cease-fire in a difficult interaction with your partner so that you can pause, de-escalate your anxiety, and regain your composure before interacting with your loved one again. For time-outs to be of maximum benefit, however, it's essential that you and your partner be on the same page regarding your plan to take time-outs. You need to explain the purpose of time-outs and the importance of taking a time-out the moment you feel anxiety escalating. Because conflict with your partner may be a trigger for your anxiety, you and your partner also need to establish a plan you can follow to initiate a time-out if you get anxious in the middle of a difficult interaction. Sticking to the plan is vital.

Your partner needs to understand that your taking a time-out is different from retreating or distancing yourself from her out of anger, fear, or hurt. Time-outs need to be understood as a *temporary* cessation of communication so that you can perform some needed self-care and return to your interaction in a more balanced way, better able to communicate and experience a sense of connection. Make sure that your partner understands that you will be taking time-outs to regulate your *internal* experience of anxiety. When you both understand that time-outs benefit you *and* your relationship, and when you are mutually committed to them, you will feel free to take a time-out whenever you need to do so.

EXERCISE 2♥2
Communicate with Your Partner

This exercise will help you introduce the concept of a time-out to your partner and establish a mutual understanding of the time-out procedure you will enact. The sample dialogue is included to walk you through this discussion and collaboration process. It's not intended to be used word for word. It's a jumping-off point from which you can formulate your own explanation. Additionally, if you get nervous while you are broaching the topic with your partner, the sample dialogue can serve as a good script on the spot.

1. Ask whether it's a good time to talk about something important: "I would like to talk to you about something that is important to me. Is this a good time for you?"

Wait for the answer. If the answer is yes, proceed; if not, ask when would be a better time. (It's better to wait if your partner is distracted or stressed.)

2. Explain the concept and the need for the time-out: "I've been learning some tools to help de-escalate my anxiety when I start to overreact. When I notice myself overreacting, I'm going to start taking 'time-outs.' They'll help me calm down, soothe myself, and better understand my reaction. Once I'm calm, I'll be more likely to respond to you from a place of reason."

3. Explain the time frame and where the time-out location will be: "The time-out will take me anywhere from five to twenty-five minutes, depending on what I need. I was thinking I'd use our bedroom for the time-out location. Is that okay with you?"

4. Share how you are going to communicate that you need a time-out: "When I need to take a time-out, I plan to say, 'I need a time-out now,' or I'll give you a time-out signal. Then I'll head straight for my time-out spot. I'm going to make a point of doing this consistently. Once I let you know I need a time-out, I'm going to stop talking with you immediately and go directly to my time-out."

5. Explain that the time-out is a temporary pause in interaction, *not* abandonment or avoidance: "I'd like you to think of my time-outs as a temporary pause in our communication. Right now, I'm committing to you that I won't use time-outs as a way of avoiding interaction with you or deflecting something that I just don't want to deal with. I'll just be taking a break for about ten or fifteen minutes to relax, and then I'll return. These time-outs will allow me to get calm and centered so that I can come back and communicate effectively, in a way that doesn't cause harm to me or you. When I come back from the time-out, we can decide when would be best to continue our conversation."

  (Remember, sticking to the signal and time-out procedure also helps ensure that the time-out is constructive to your relationship, rather than a way to avoid conversation or confrontation with your partner.)

6. Seal the deal: "Is this plan okay with you? Does it make sense? Do you have any thoughts or suggestions on how to make it work better for us? I am open to your feedback and want to collaborate so that this method can work well for us."

The Time-Out: Practicing Self-Soothing Techniques

Once you're in your time-out location, you can use a variety of self-soothing techniques to defuse your anxiety. This chapter teaches six quick and efficient ways to calm your body and mind, each of which has a distinct effect:

- *Closed eye roll:* Quickly interrupts a reaction

- *Tight fist:* Releases muscular tension

- *Four-square breathing:* Helps you self-soothe with calming breath

- Heavy arms, heavy legs: Creates calm

- *Warm belly, cool forehead:* Increases your sense of calm

- *Fast-forward to the future:* Propels you to anticipate relief

These techniques ease your anxiety so that you can return from your time-outs in a calm, balanced state. The following section will teach you how to practice the six exercises. We suggest that you do the techniques sequentially in your time-outs, but nothing is set in stone. You can use as many or as few of them as you need to regain a sense of calm. Likewise, there's no set duration for a time-out; it might be as short as two or three minutes, or as long as twenty minutes. The key is to give yourself as long as you need to restore your equilibrium. On any given day, at any given moment, the length of time you need for a time-out is likely to vary.

Quickly Interrupting a Reaction

This technique is inspired by two leaders in the field of clinical hypnosis: Herbert Spiegel and Dabney Ewin. Although Dr. Spiegel initially used eye rolls to help assess a person's ability to be hypnotized (Spiegel and Spiegel 1978), it's a quick (taking less than a minute), powerful tool to help you focus your attention and de-escalate heightened levels of anxiety the minute you enter into your time-out. Although you can do the eye roll with your eyes open, in this method you keep your eyes closed, as recommended by Dr. Ewin (pers. comm.). This will be important when you learn how to apply the eye roll during interactions with your partner (see chapter 5). However, you can do the remaining exercises taught in this chapter with your eyes open or closed, based on your personal preference.

EXERCISE 2.3
Closed Eye Roll

To practice the eye roll, read the following four easy steps before closing your eyes and performing them.

1. Close your eyes and look as far upward as you can.

2. Breathe in deeply as you hold your eyes upward. It's as if you were trying to see if your eyes could actually reach the highest point on the arc of your eyebrows. You may experience a sensation of tension in your eyeballs along with a relaxed feeling in the eyelids—this is normal. Or you might just be aware of the stretching of your eye muscles.

3. Hold your eyes in this position for about ten or fifteen seconds, welcoming the sensations of both tension and stretching that you feel in the muscles surrounding your eye sockets.

4. Exhale, and at the same time, relax your eyes—perhaps in a moment feeling that the relaxation in your eyes is spreading to other parts of your body.

Releasing Muscular Tension

The tight-fist exercise is based on the reality that our bodies and minds are containers for our emotions. Worry, fear, and anxiety manifest as thoughts, emotions, and physical sensations that include muscle tension. In the following exercise, you pair visualization with the simple movement of clenching and releasing your fist in order to release muscle tension and promote a sense of calm and ease. You can release muscular tension in a matter of minutes as you simultaneously discharge fear or worry.

The tight-fist exercise is a gentle way to acknowledge your anxiety and to build and hold the tension until your body and mind are primed to release it. In fact, the exercise capitalizes on your natural tendency to heighten your anxiety—only now you can use this tendency to bring about relaxation and relief. Finally, this technique relaxes your muscles, which will help you practice the exercise that comes after this one, four-square breathing.

EXERCISE 2.4
Tight Fist

We suggest reading through the following steps a few times to familiarize yourself with the procedure and then performing them from memory.

1. Gather your tension:
   First, imagine that all of your uncomfortable emotions—fear, panic, worry, irritability, agitation—are traveling into one of your hands. Take as much time as you need to let all of your emotions gather in this small space in your body.

2. Focus your attention:
   Direct your attention to the hand in which your emotions are collecting.

3. Tense:
   When you can feel that your hand is filled with the tension and energy, slowly make a fist with that hand. Tighten the fist more and more, until you are squeezing it as tightly as you can.

4. Transform tension to liquid:
   Now imagine that all the tension in that hand turns to liquid, in a color of your own choosing. This colored liquid represents your distress, worry, and other uncomfortable emotions. As you allow the tension to morph into this colored liquid, notice how much effort and energy it takes to hold that tension so tightly in your fist. Maybe the muscles in your hand and arm are becoming tired. Maybe they are beginning to ache a bit. Maybe your hand or arm is beginning to shake or tremble ever so slightly, as your muscles begin to tire from the continued effort of squeezing your tension so tightly.

5. Relax your fist:
   As you feel the exhaustion in the muscles in your hand and arm, gradually ease into the relaxation, the release that your body needs. Ever so slowly, allow the muscles in your fingers, your thumb, your palm, and your wrist to ease their grip.

6. Release the tension:
   Imagine the colored liquid in your hand flowing to the floor at whatever speed feels right. See the liquid flowing straight through the floor, down into the ground. Imagine that it's being absorbed deep into the earth, where it is cleansed and released

far away from you. And now, sense the stillness, the comfort, the relief that completely permeates each muscle in your hand after holding the tension for so long. And you might even take a deep breath in, breathing a sigh of relief at the release of this tension.

7. Close:
End this exercise by shaking your hand a bit as you count backward from five to one. When you get to one, allow yourself to enjoy feeling relaxed, refreshed, and alert. And know that at any future time, you can direct your body to release unnecessary tension in just a couple of minutes.

Soothing Yourself with Calming Breath

Like the beating of our hearts or the coursing of blood through our veins, breathing is something that our bodies do automatically. Since breathing is such a basic, constant part of our existence, we rarely focus on it. This makes sense: imagine having to focus on each individual inhalation and exhalation as you walk through the grocery store, compose an e-mail, or carry on a conversation. If breathing required conscious attention, it would be very hard to get anything done and impossible to get any sleep.

Attending to and changing the breath, however, can help you quickly de-escalate anxiety responses. When you become anxious, many of the muscles in your body tense. This can include muscles that affect the movement of the diaphragm and rib cage, which in turn affect your breathing. So the increased muscle tension that accompanies anxiety often leads to shallow, restricted breathing. That, in turn, can then lead to greater anxiety, because your intake of oxygen and release of carbon dioxide—both of which are essential to a feeling of well-being—are reduced.

Breathing exercises that get you breathing deeply and slowly can quickly defuse an anxiety response. Four-square breathing is one of our favorite breathing exercises, because it's quick and simple. All it requires is the ability to count to four. You will use this breathing technique in your time-outs and during your interactions with your partner (see chapter 5).

EXERCISE 2.5
Four-Square Breathing

Select a chair or couch on which you can sit upright comfortably, with your spine straight and your feet flat on the floor. This posture enhances your ability to engage in calming, deep breathing. After you have read through the following steps and suggestions, you can perform them from memory:

1. Inhale to the count of four (one second per count).

2. Hold your breath to the count of four.

3. Exhale to the count of four.

4. Hold your breath to the count of four.

Repeat this cycle. There's no set number of minutes for repetitions, and it's usually beneficial to do this exercise for one to three minutes at a time. If you have trouble making it to the count of four, use a count of three.

Adding a visualization component to four-square breathing can help keep your brain busy, directing your attention to the exercise and leaving less room for worried thoughts to creep in. You might experiment with adding the following simple visualization to accompany the breathing pattern.

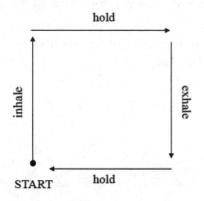

1. As you breathe in to the count of four, visualize yourself drawing a vertical line, upward, starting at the left-bottom corner of an imaginary square.

2. As you hold your breath to the count of four, visualize yourself drawing the top of the square from left to right.

3. As you exhale to the count of four, draw the right side of the square by extending the line downward.

4. As you hold your breath to the count of four, complete the square by drawing the bottom line from right to left.

When you begin the next repetition of the breath cycle, you can also begin drawing a new square.

Creating and Increasing Calm

The next two techniques consistently elicit an optimal level of calm, often in just a few minutes. They are adapted from a relaxation approach called *autogenic training*, which is based on the understanding that your words and imagination influence your body's reaction to stress. Johannes Schultz, the German psychiatrist and neurologist who developed autogenic training, found that the relaxation response is characteristically accompanied by certain physical sensations, including a sensation of coolness throughout the forehead, along with heaviness and warmth in the extremities and abdomen (Luthe and Schultz 1969). The sensations of heaviness and warmth generated in the following two autogenic training exercises are associated with two physiological phenomena: falling asleep and the calming of the fight-or-flight response (in other words, the engagement of the parasympathetic nervous system). You may not notice it, but when you are ready to sleep, your body becomes very still and your limbs become heavy. So with the "heavy arms, heavy legs" exercise, you are communicating to your body and mind that it's safe to let go of unnecessary vigilance and fear; you are telling your brain that it's safe to let go of anxiety.

When you experience fight-or-flight response, the blood flow is directed to the muscles and organs that will most effectively mobilize your body to either fight or flee. So, for example, your calves and biceps receive greater-than-average blood flow, while your fingers and toes receive less. Your gastrointestinal tract, which includes the stomach, also receives less blood flow than average. (During fight and flight, digestion is not a priority.) This diminished blood flow is often accompanied by sensations of cold. The warmth generated in your extremities and abdomen in the following exercises will counter the sensations your body associates with the fight-or-flight response. Warm hands and a warm belly signal to the body that everything is safe. They also tell the brain that it's safe to let go of anxiety.

As you practice the following two calming exercises, you might also notice that as the heaviness and warmth increase, your breath and heart rate gradually become slower and more regular. These are signs of increasing calm as your parasympathetic nervous system puts the brakes on your anxiety response. In mere minutes you can shift from pushing the gas to pumping the brakes when you use these two interventions to balance your autonomic nervous system.

EXERCISE 2.6
Heavy Arms, Heavy Legs

For this exercise, we suggest that you first read through the following steps and then do them from memory. To begin, find a comfortable position on a chair or couch in a quiet place.

1. Focus on your right hand and imagine that it's becoming heavy. You can imagine that there's a lead weight on your hand. Then say to yourself three times, *My right hand is heavy.*

2. Imagine the heaviness spreading past your wrist, up your arm, and all the way to your shoulder. Then say to yourself three times, *My right arm is heavy.*

3. Shift your attention to your left hand and repeat the same sequence. Then feel both your arms, sensing their weight, their heaviness.

4. Shift your attention to your legs. Imagine your lower right leg and your right foot getting very heavy, and say to yourself three times, *My right foot and leg are heavy.*

    And now imagine that there are thirty-pound sandbags on your right thigh, and feel the heaviness as you say to yourself three times, *My whole right leg is heavy.*

5. Repeat the sequence in step four with your left foot and leg.

By the time you've completed the sequences, your body will be relaxed and your anxiety eased.

EXERCISE 2.7
Warm Belly, Cool Forehead

This technique increases the relaxation response you achieved with the previous exercise. A warm stomach is a calm stomach, and a calm stomach sends messages to your whole body that you are safe and comfortable. Like the previous exercise, this exercise uses your imagination and words to create the desired response.

1. Focus on your stomach and abdomen area, and imagine that it is getting warm. Let your stomach become just as warm as needed for you to be comfortable. Notice, too, that your arms and legs are still heavy, and that now you have the pleasurable experience of a warm center as well. Allow these pleasurable sensations to increase.

2. Shift your attention to your forehead. Imagine a cool breeze brushing across it or, if you prefer, imagine a cold compress cooling your forehead, helping you keep a cool head. Repeat to yourself, *My forehead is cool* and *I think clearly with a cool head*.

3. You can close this exercise by shaking your arms and legs lightly, becoming alert again, but with a calm body. As you do so, remind yourself that you can return to this calm, comfortable state whenever you wish.

Anticipating Relief

Future focusing, as we discussed in chapter 1, is at the heart of anxiety-prone reaction styles. In the following exercise, you can use your natural tendency to focus on the future to *reduce* your anxiety. No matter how overwhelming your anxiety feels when it crops up, there is one absolute: it will pass. There will be a time, often just minutes into the future, when your surging heartbeat will settle back to its calm, soft, rhythmic thumps. Your worried thoughts will dissipate as life progresses, moment by moment, second by second. When you are consumed by fear or worry, it's helpful to remember that this excruciating sensation is time limited, and as time passes, it will fade.

EXERCISE 2.8
Fast-Forward to the Future

When you are flooded with anxiety, fear is often all that you can see. This simple fast-forwarding technique can cue you to step back and gain the assurance that although you are currently experiencing fear, you will soon be alright.

If you've been doing the exercises in this section sequentially during your time-out as suggested, by the time you reach this exercise, your anxiety has likely already diminished significantly as a result of practicing the calming techniques. We've found that this final relaxation exercise is especially helpful to complete just before you end your time-out. As with the previous exercises, after you have read through the following steps and suggestions, you can perform them from memory.

1. Begin by taking a moment to conceptualize the linear progression of time: see your day progressing from beginning to end.

2. Imagine that your whole day is now recorded on a video and you hold the remote control that allows you to pause, fast-forward, or play the recording of your day.

3. In your mind's eye, pause the current scene—the one in which you are experiencing heightened anxiety.

4. Now tap the fast-forward button to skip to the next scene in your day.

5. Finally, hit the play button and see yourself in the very near future: calm, serene, and okay. The panic, anxiety, or worry has passed, and you are engaged calmly and productively in the activities of your day.

On completing this last exercise of the time-out, you probably feel calm and at ease. In the unlikely event that there's some remaining stress, simply repeat the sequence of exercises until your anxiety has lessened. And when you are ready, you can leave your time-out space and resume your normal activities.

Wrapping It Up

As you recognize your triggers, use time-outs to lessen your anxiety, and practice the exercises in this chapter, you will become more and more skilled at shifting from anxiety to calmness. Anxiety will no longer have the power it once did to negatively affect your life and your relationship. To recap, the three steps of the time-out are as follows:

1. Recognize when you're triggered.

2. Initiate a time-out.

3. Engage in self-soothing techniques:

   1. Closed eye roll: Quickly interrupts a reaction

   2. Tight fist: Releases muscular tension

   3. Four-square breathing: Soothes you with calming breath

   4. Heavy arms, heavy legs: Creates calm

   5. Warm belly, cool forehead: Increases calm

   6. Fast-forward to the future: Helps you anticipate relief

Although implementing your time-outs requires discipline, it's well worth the effort. In addition to gaining a means of regulating your anxiety, you are altering the way that you and your partner interact. Rather than continuing to engage with your partner as your anxiety escalates or looking to your partner to regulate your anxiety, *you* now hold the reins. You—and your relationship—are no longer at the mercy of your anxiety.

In the next chapter, you will learn how to enhance your new ability to manage your anxiety with a number of techniques that lessen your overall anxiety levels. With the time-out tools in hand, you can defuse intense anxiety *when it arises*. Next, you will create a daily relaxation regimen that will diminish your baseline levels of anxiety as well.

chapter 3

Lowering Your Baseline Level of Anxiety: The Daily Stress Inoculation

"I'm always so antsy in the mornings," said Paul, a fifty-eight-year-old attorney. "Before my hand hits the alarm, I'm thinking about all the things I need to do—even if it's the weekend. I want to jump up and get started. The longer I wait to start the tasks of my day, the jumpier I get. Until the other morning, I had forgotten that my life didn't used to be like that.

"When we first bought our house, Mary and I used to get up thirty minutes early each morning so we could take our time and enjoy breakfast and coffee together before officially starting our day. But then we started having kids, and I became busy trying to make partner in the law firm. Then I made partner, and my demands at work increased even more. Now I'm always rushing somewhere or checking e-mail and voice mail. If my phone isn't buzzing with incoming mail or an incoming call, I'm waiting for the moment when it will.

"I'd forgotten our morning ritual until Mary made me breakfast for our twenty-fifth anniversary a few days ago. She really fussed over it, making my favorite pancakes and setting the table beautifully. And I have to admit: I didn't enjoy it as I used to. I rushed through breakfast and even fielded an e-mail on my PDA while we were at the table. And the second we were done with breakfast, I hopped up to get ready for work. She took it personally, as if I didn't appreciate the effort she had made and didn't want to spend time with her. She complained that I'm always preoccupied or in a hurry. We ended up getting into a fight over it. Mary said that now that the kids are out of the house, she'd been looking forward to spending *more* time with me, not less.

"I *want* to spend time with Mary! It's just that I can't seem to slow down these days, even when I want to. I'm always worried that I'm not going to get everything done, so when I try to slow down, I get really anxious. I wish Mary were more understanding about the pressure I'm under. There's no way I could possibly relax with a leisurely breakfast before work anymore."

Paul and Mary's problem isn't unique for couples in which one partner suffers from anxiety. Paul's future-focus on his anticipated demands of the day interfered with his ability to relax and connect with his wife on the morning of their wedding anniversary. His anxiety, however, affected far more than his ability to enjoy their anniversary breakfast. It became a source of conflict between him and his wife. Mary frequently interpreted Paul's rushing and multitasking as a lack of interest in their relationship. While this was far from the case, Paul's heightened anxiety *did* interfere with his ability to connect with his wife.

This is a common problem for couples with one chronically anxious partner. If your baseline anxiety level is set to "red alert" while your partner's baseline is on "green," your relationship will suffer. For your individual well-being and for the well-being of your relationship, it's essential that you learn how to decrease your baseline stress levels. The following daily stress inoculation will help you achieve this.

The Daily Stress Inoculation

The daily stress inoculation builds on the relaxation tools you learned for your time-outs in chapter 2. After doing the self-soothing techniques (exercises 2.3 through 2.7), you simply add two new exercises, each of which has a distinct effect:

- *Safe-place meditation:* Creates a sense of safety.

- *Closing affirmations:* Cements your success.

By setting aside as little as twenty minutes each day to practice these eight techniques, you can lower your baseline level of stress and prevent damage to your relationship.

Benefits of the Daily Stress Inoculation

Teaching your mind and body to "gear down," so to speak, has three major benefits: recalibrating stress-hormone levels, producing optimal brain-wave activity, and enhancing the effectiveness of your time-outs.

Recalibrating Stress-Hormone Levels

The daily stress inoculation is, first and foremost, geared to reduce your baseline levels of stress, anxiety, and tension. However, chronic anxiety leads to elevated levels of stress hormones that circulate throughout your body. This can cause you to feel more keyed up and anxious. You'll recall that in some of the anxiety disorders, these chronically elevated levels of stress hormones can cause physical discomforts such as muscle tension, tension headaches, and gastrointestinal upsets.

Practicing the daily stress inoculation can help decrease the amount of stress hormones released into your system and increase the release of *serotonin*, a neurochemical linked to positive mood. In effect, you're shifting your internal homeostasis. Just as your body keeps your temperature hovering around 98 degrees, chronic anxiety keeps your stress levels hovering at the equivalent of 101 degrees—hurried, feverish. With regular repetition, the daily stress inoculation allows your body and mind to recalibrate your "stress temperature" by altering the concentrations of neurochemicals and hormones in your system.

Producing Optimal Brain-Wave Activity

Engaging in the daily stress inoculation can also produce beneficial brain-wave activity. Different states of mind are associated with different types of brain waves. Beta waves are associated with anxiety and worry, while alpha and theta waves are associated with states of calm and relaxation. The daily stress inoculation shifts your brain from the buzzing busyness of beta-wave activity to calm, tranquil alpha and theta rhythms. You're literally teaching your brain to function at a different pace.

Enhancing the Effectiveness of Your Time-Outs

The daily stress inoculation's repetition of the exercises from your time-out routine has another benefit: as you generate a state of calm during your stress inoculation, you're also becoming more skilled at your time-out exercises. The more you practice the self-soothing exercises in the daily stress inoculation, the better able you will be to quickly and easily induce a state of relaxation and well-being, no matter where you are or what you encounter. With the daily stress inoculation, you're both lowering your stress levels *and* ensuring that the anxiety-reducing tools at your command are all the more powerful.

The Steps of the Daily Stress Inoculation

Once you decide where to practice your daily stress inoculation (your time-out spot at home would work perfectly), begin by doing the first five exercises of your time-out protocol:

1. Closed eye roll (exercise 2.3)

2. Tight fist (exercise 2.4)

3. Four-square breathing (exercise 2.5)

4. Heavy arms, heavy legs (exercise 2.6)

5. Warm belly, cool forehead (exercise 2.7)

After doing these exercises, proceed with the following two new exercises, safe place and closing affirmations.

Creating a Sense of Safety

The safe-place exercise uses imagination and visualization to help you self-soothe. By imagining being in a soothing place, you can quickly shift your body and mind to a state of calm. Some people like to select a particular safe place, perhaps a vacation spot they especially enjoyed. Others use different images, depending on what appeals to them on any given day. Many people are drawn to water and have fond memories of relaxing on a beach. Others are soothed by images of mountains, forests, valleys, or gardens. Still others prefer to go to an imaginary safe room that they create to their specifications. The key to successful visualization is incorporating all the senses. The more details you include of what you see, hear, smell, and feel in your safe place, the more real it becomes to you. And the more real it feels, the more likely it is that your safe place will have a powerful calming effect on you.

EXERCISE 3.1
Safe Place or Safe Room

The following scripts and steps will guide you through creating and then accessing your safe place. You can use two different scripts for the creation phase. The first leads you to create a safe space in nature; the second helps you create a safe room. If you know that you prefer one setting over the other, simply skip the script that doesn't spark your interest. If you're not sure what setting you want, give both visualizations a try. Your ideal safe place that you discover through these meditations might surprise you.

Because the scripts for the safe-place meditations are longer than previous ones, we suggest that you prepare for the exercise by either recording the scripts or asking a friend, your therapist, or your partner to read them to you. Then find a quiet, comfortable place (your daily stress inoculation space would work perfectly); get yourself in a relaxed, centered state of mind with the closed eye roll (exercise 2.3) and a few four-square breaths (exercise 2.5); and allow the following words to guide you.

Safe Place: A Scene in Nature

Now that you've accessed a sense of calm with the closed eye roll and a few four-square breaths, you can continue to relax and enjoy connecting to an image and experience that will deepen your relaxation. Sit in the stillness of your inner world for a moment and ask yourself where in nature you would like to be. You can go anywhere you'd like. It could be somewhere you've been before or somewhere you would like to go, somewhere real or somewhere in your imagination. It could be a place you remember from the recent past or from long ago in your childhood. Let your intuition guide you to just the right place.

Once you've selected the place that feels right, allow yourself to go there now, mentally perceiving this place with all of your senses. Look around and see your safe place with your inner eye. Some people can create vivid pictures in their mind's eye, while others only see things dimly or partially—both are okay.

All that matters is that you get some inner sense of your safe place as you look at the surroundings of the place you have chosen. And what do you hear? Can you sense sounds, sounds that are soothing, sounds that you hear with your inner ear: perhaps the sounds of surf—or breeze or music—or maybe laughter?

And the sense of smell is so powerful. You know what it feels like, don't you?—to smell something that brings you right back to a place, a time, or an experience that was wonderful? Allow yourself, now, to really connect with all the scents you associate
with your safe place.

And what does it feel like to be in your safe place? Is there a breeze on your face, the warmth of the sun? Can you feel sand or grass under your feet? Perhaps you can mentally reach out and touch something there? A leaf, a flower, the bark on a tree? Are you sitting down or walking? Or perhaps lying back on a beach chair or blanket?

And you can enjoy the stillness as you connect to your safe place—allowing yourself to fully experience your safe place. Just attend to what it feels like to be there, and you can stay there for as long as you wish…nurtured by nature, nurtured by stillness, connected to the beauty that you can create with your imagination.

And to make it easy for you to return to your safe place, you can create a cue that will automatically bring you back to your safe place with a lovely feeling of peace in your body and mind. To create this cue, select a phrase that will remind you of where you are. Some people, for example, might select the phrase "ocean of calm" if their safe place is by the sea; others might say "majestic mountain" if their safe place is in the mountains. And now take a moment to let your own phrase come to mind, a phrase that signifies the safe place you have just created for yourself. This phrase doesn't even have to logically make sense; let it be whatever feels right to you. And once your phrase has come to mind, allow yourself to pick a freeze-frame image of your safe place and repeat your phrase to yourself while seeing this singular image vividly in your mind's eye.

And by anchoring this phrase and picture, you are training your brain to very quickly push the replay button. And when you press this replay button with this phrase and image, the good feelings will come back automatically—automatically and quickly. So it will be very easy for you to elicit this wonderful place and the calm feelings that accompany it. And you can look forward to returning to your safe place again and again—pleased to discover that your safe place is accessible to you in your imagination, always available to you whenever you wish to revisit it and bring its soothing benefits back to you. And when you're ready to leave your safe place, knowing that you can always return, you can count slowly from one to twenty, taking all the time you need to open your eyes.

Safe Place: Creating a Safe Room

Rather than a safe place in nature, you may want to create a safe room. Simply use the following guidance (adapted with permission of W. W. Norton and Company from Carolyn's 2007 book *Affect Regulation Toolbox: Practical and Effective Hypnotic Interventions for the Over-Reactive Client*).

Now that you've accessed a sense of calm with a closed
eye roll and a few four-square breaths, you can continue
to relax—relax and enjoy connecting to an image and
experience that will deepen your relaxation as you use the
power of your imagination to visualize a special room—
a safe room, a retreat room—a room that is comforting,
soothing…where you can go to relax. Look around this
room, and as you do, enjoy decorating it so that it will be
especially pleasing and comforting for you. Take some
time to decorate the room just as you'd like. You are the
creator, the designer of this imaginary room, so perhaps
you can take special enjoyment in selecting the decor—
furnishing it however you like—with just the right colors,
just the right textures, just the right furnishings that are
pleasing to you.

Can you see the colors, hear the sounds, and feel the
feelings you'd like to feel in this room? Look around your
room…perhaps now you might like to sit down in a comfortable chair or on a couch or to lie down on a bed—
taking particular enjoyment in discovering how nice
it is to sit or lie down…and to rest. And as you mentally
sense yourself relaxing—in this lovely room—you can
experience a feeling of soothing comfort. Isn't it a pleasure
to have a room of your own, where you can rest, dream,
attend to a growing sense of peace—far away from
your everyday concerns? And now, focusing back inside
your room again, what soothing sounds do you hear?
The crackling of logs in a fireplace? The breeze coming
through a window? Soft music playing in the background?
The light trickling of a small indoor fountain?

Take a moment to enjoy your sanctuary—this room
of yours, this place of peace and comfort that you have
created. And also enjoy your mind's capacity to create a
feeling of calm and peace just by using your imagination.

And you can look forward to returning to this safe,
sheltering room whenever you wish—knowing that this

room and its nurturing qualities are always available to you anytime you wish to return.

And to make it easier for you to return to your safe room, you can create a cue that will automatically bring you back to your special place with a lovely feeling of peace in your body and mind. To create this anchor or cue so that your mind and body will remember your safe room, select a word or phrase that will remind you of this special place. Some people might select the word "sunroom," for example, if their safe room is filled with warm sunlight; others might choose the phrase "soft room" if their safe place is filled with soft furniture and carpeting.

Now take a moment to let your own word or phrase come to mind, one that signifies the safe place you have just created for yourself. This phrase doesn't even have to make sense logically; let it be whatever feels right to you. And once your phrase has come to mind, allow yourself to pick a freeze-frame image of your safe room, as you repeat your phrase to yourself while seeing this singular image vividly in your mind's eye.

By anchoring this phrase and image, you are training your brain to very quickly push the replay button so that the good feelings will come back automatically—and quickly. So it will be very easy for you to elicit this wonderful place and the calm feelings that accompany it. And you can look forward to returning to your safe room again and again during your daily stress inoculation— pleased to discover that your safe room is accessible to you in your imagination, always available to you whenever you wish to revisit it and bring its soothing benefits back to you. And when you're ready to leave your safe room, knowing that you can always return, you can count slowly from one to twenty, taking all the time you need to open your eyes.

Accessing Your Safe Place

Now that you have created your safe place, you can access it not only in the daily stress inoculation, but also whenever you wish to take a short break, relax, and bring back the soothing feelings and images associated with your safe place. You can use the following quick-and-easy three-step protocol to access your safe place.

1. Close your eyes and repeat your cue phrase to yourself while recalling your freeze-frame image of your safe place.

2. Allow this cue to bring you back to your safe place, recalling the sights, sounds, smells, and sensations associated with this place.

3. Focus on the feelings of safety and comfort, holding on to these feelings as you relax in your safe space for about five minutes. If you notice your mind wandering during this time, repeat your cue phrase and gently bring your attention back to the sights and sensations of your safe place, paying particular attention to the accompanying feelings of well-being.

Cementing Your Success with Closing Affirmations

The words that we say to ourselves hold power. Emile Coué (1922), a renowned French pharmacist who practiced hypnosis in the early twentieth century, asserted that any idea exclusively occupying the mind turns into reality. In this light, we conclude the daily stress inoculation with a set of affirmations that reinforce, enhance, and celebrate the commitment you have made to yourself by engaging in this daily practice.

EXERCISE 3.2
Closing Affirmations

Still enjoying the sense of well-being brought about by your safe-place experience, read through the following statements a few times. Then close your eyes and repeat each of them three times, either out loud or silently, even if you feel that they are only partially true.

I've taken time for myself.

I've taken time to honor my need to attend to myself.

I've taken time to open myself to relaxation, stillness, and receptivity.

I am balanced.

I am resilient.

I've accessed stillness and calm.

If there are any other affirming statements that feel right for you, feel free to add them. You can also repeat any of the affirmations more than three times if you'd like.

At the end of your final affirmation, take one deep inhalation and exhalation, and say to yourself, *I am ready to go on with my day in this calm, peaceful state.*

Making the Daily Stress Inoculation a Habit

Over the years, we have seen the daily stress-reduction exercises bring about such startling benefits that we strongly encourage everyone with heightened anxiety to begin a daily practice. Even if the last thing you feel like doing is putting away your to-do list, turning off the phone, and shutting down your computer to do the daily stress inoculation, it's still well worth putting in the time for self-care. There's a big difference between *wanting* to do something that's good for you and actually *doing* it. Incorporating a new routine or practice into your daily life means changing old habits and creating new ones. If you've ever tried going on a diet or adding physical exercise to your weekly routine, it's likely that you've already discovered this simple truth: changing your habits can be tough. To address this challenge, the final section of this chapter is dedicated to helping you form a new habit so that the daily stress inoculation can become a routine part of your day—as routine as brushing your teeth in the morning, something that you automatically do without giving it a second thought.

There's always a reason *not* to relax—especially if you're someone who experiences chronic anxiety. However, it's important that you make this practice a routine part of your daily life. The following two exercises will help you make the daily stress inoculation a habit:

- *Accessing the wise parent within:* Helps you connect with a part of yourself that is strong and encouraging.

- *Visualizing adhering to your daily stress inoculation:* Helps you harness your power of intention.

Accessing Inner Strength

To overcome any resistance you might have to daily practice, it's helpful to connect to a part of yourself that we call *the wise parent.* Your wise parent is your *ideal* parent: a strong, nurturing part of you that is both firm and encouraging. It's a mature part of you; it's your strong, compassionate, and kind self. It speaks to you in a soft voice and is always available to you when you need to recall the wisdom you have accumulated in your life. This wise parent can guide the younger parts of you—the more impulsive parts that vie for instant gratification—to take action that's in your best interest. Like any good parent, this wise parent sets clear expectations with kindness, compassion, and patience.

Regardless of the kind of parenting you actually had as a child, you can access this firm and compassionate part of yourself. Doing so enables you to acknowledge all the desires, feelings, and impulses that might tempt you *not* to do your daily practice, and still do your daily stress inoculation anyway.

EXERCISE 3.3
Access the Wise Parent Within

To prepare for this wise-parent exercise, take some time to familiarize yourself with the following script. Alternatively, record the script, or have a friend or therapist agree to read it to you. Once you are ready to begin, get into a relaxed state by doing the closed eye roll (exercise 2.3) and a few rounds of four-square breathing (exercise 2.5). When you feel calm and centered, proceed with the following script.

As you sit quietly, take a moment to get in touch with your wise parent within. Begin by remembering a time when you comforted a child or advised a friend or coworker—a time when you offered someone wise counsel or good judgment, when you trusted your instincts and enjoyed sharing from this mature, caring part of yourself. Remember where you were, whom you were with, and how you spoke to this person. And as you access this memory and hold it in your mind, sense what your body felt like as you held the position of a kind, sturdy, caring figure for another—notice the way you carried yourself in that encounter. Sense how you experienced yourself when you offered wisdom, when you were in touch with this wise parent part of yourself. Pay attention to how your body felt as you remember. Perhaps you could feel your spine, strong and stable, your feet firmly anchored on the ground. And now bring your awareness of this strong self into the present. Feel that same strength in your spine, and carry back with you the calmness and sense of solidity that comes as you access that kind, knowing figure that lives within.

The heart of your wise self values your health and well-being. So with your parent self at the forefront of your awareness, gently tell yourself how important it is to attend to the discipline of a daily self-soothing practice. You might sense resistance from those younger parts of you, which may feel distracted or lazy or unwilling. Sometimes this resistance is small and easily managed. Sometimes it is tough—and rigid—and requires some extra firmness. This is a kind of gentle, moderate yet firm guidance to help the more resistant part of you do what you know is in your best interest.

The more you get in touch with your wise parent, the easier it is for that part of you to influence your thoughts, your reactions, and your emotions. And the more frequently your wise parent is at the helm, the more likely it is that you'll build and adhere to the habits you wish to incorporate into your daily life—habits that will soften your anxiety, improve your interactions with your partner, and ultimately change your baseline levels of stress. So when you notice that resistance crop up and that you are feeling those younger, lazy, or undisciplined parts of yourself calling the shots, access the wise parent within and say to yourself with firmness and compassion, I know you don't feel like doing this, but you're going to do it anyway because it's good for you.

Harnessing the Power of Intention

The power of intention is immense. When you tap into the power of your intentions, you give new meaning to the phrase "seeing is believing": by visualizing and sensing yourself engaging in an activity, you enhance the likelihood that you will actually *do* the activity. In the following exercise, you will use visualization to help harness the power of your good intentions and enhance your commitment to, and enthusiasm for, your daily stress inoculation.

Some of us are more visually oriented and others more kinesthetically (or touch) oriented. As you do the following guided visualization, don't worry if your visual images or physical sensations are not as vivid as you'd like. People vary concerning which senses are easier to access. For example, when asked to imagine a sunset, a visually oriented person might describe the vivid pinks and purples of a sunset at the beach. A more kinesthetically oriented person would describe the cool breeze brushing across his face and the warmth of the setting sun. The following visualization includes a wealth of both visual and kinesthetic detail, so regardless of your particular strength, you can have a powerful experience.

EXERCISE 3.4
Visualize Sticking to Your Daily Stress Inoculation

We suggest you do this visualization just before going to bed at night, as you anticipate the possibilities the next day can bring. After you've familiarized yourself with the following script or alternatively made preparations to have it read to you or to play a recording of it, get comfortable in your bed and proceed. As you do the visualization, remember that you aren't actually doing the exercises, but *imagining* yourself doing them.

As you lie in the comfort of your bed, close your eyes, take a couple of slow breaths, and begin to imagine yourself at the time tomorrow that you have set aside for your daily stress inoculation. In your mind's eye, see yourself sitting in the space you've chosen for your daily practice, wherever that might be. Maybe you're sitting in your favorite comfortable chair. Or maybe you're on the couch or on a mat, propped up with pillows in your home or office. And now allow yourself to begin to sense what it's like to occupy this space. Imagine what it feels like to sit on your chair or floor or couch—how the chair or couch or mat is supporting your body.

And now that you see yourself there, watch in your mind's eye as you begin your daily stress inoculation. See yourself closing your eyes to begin the closed eye roll, one small gesture that signifies the start of lowering your baseline stress level for good. Next, fast-forward in time to see yourself having completed the tight-fist exercise and beginning your four-square breathing. See your chest rise with each inhalation and sense how, with each new breath, you are infusing yourself with a sense of calm.

Now fast-forward to the end of your "heavy arms, heavy legs" and "warm belly, cool forehead" exercises. Imagine the comfort in your body, the shifts in your posture, as a sense of serenity and calm continues to permeate your entire being. Feel the pleasure of having taken time out of your day to create this sensation, this feeling of inner harmony and calm that you very much deserve.

And imagine this sense of calm getting stronger and deeper as you continue your safe-place visualization and closing affirmations. And now fast-forward to the end of the closing affirmations. Feel your sense of accomplishment. Sense the satisfaction and clarity, mingling with the sense of calm and ease that comes with the knowledge that you have honored your very important commitment to do the daily inoculation. Imagine your delight at discovering that it was a very enjoyable and natural experience.

Perhaps, right now, you can let yourself enjoy anticipating how good you will feel tomorrow as you go through your daily stress inoculation, giving yourself time to balance your nervous system and create inner harmony, calm, and ease. So now promise yourself that you will take time tomorrow for that soothing break. And starting tomorrow, you can look forward to the benefits that will come to you as you consistently incorporate a self-soothing practice into your daily routine.

Wrapping It Up

With this chapter under your belt, you have the tools you need to lower your baseline level of anxiety. You also have tools that will enable you to push through any resistance to establishing and maintaining the habit of your daily stress inoculation. In the words of Aristotle, "We are what we repeatedly do. Excellence then is not an act but a habit."

We encourage you to make the daily stress inoculation a habit. Just as you lose muscle tone and stamina when you discontinue an exercise routine, your baseline level of anxiety will begin to creep upward again if you stop your daily de-stressing routine. So, once daily, remember to practice these seven simple exercises in the following order:

1. Closed eye roll (exercise 2.3): Quickly interrupts a reaction.

2. Tight fist (exercise 2.4): Releases muscular tension.

3. Four-square breathing (exercise 2.5): Helps you soothe yourself with calming breath.

4. Heavy arms, heavy legs (exercise 2.6): Creates calm.

5. Warm belly, cool forehead (exercise 2.7): Increases calm.

6. Safe-place meditation (exercise 3.1): Creates a sense of safety.

7. Closing affirmations (exercise 3.2): Helps you enhance and celebrate your success.

With routine practice of the daily stress inoculation, you can tap into inner resources you never knew you had. At the same time, as your baseline anxiety level lowers, your anxiety won't be a source of stress in your relationship. On the contrary, as you keep fueling this source of internal well-being, you'll be able to turn your attention away from possible sources of anxiety and toward creating a stronger, more intimate connection with your partner. The next two parts of this book will give you the tools to do just that.

part 2

CONNECTING WITH THE ONE YOU LOVE

chapter 4

Understanding Your Partner

In part 1 you learned about the different anxiety disorders and the toll they can take on an individual. You also learned a variety of self-soothing techniques to calm your body and mind and to increase your resiliency to stress. However, anxiety can damage your relationship as well as you. Now that you are better able to regulate your own levels of anxiety, you are ready to broaden your recovery to encompass your relationship with your partner. This chapter provides a foundation on which you can begin to recognize and repair the disconnect that may exist between you and your partner and to shift the overall dynamic of your relationship.

You may feel that if your partner really loved you, she would intuitively know how to respond to your needs and would always give you the support that you want. While this is an understandable desire, sadly it's more fantasy than likelihood. Love doesn't automatically lead to understanding or to the ability to recognize and respond sensitively to one another's needs. This is especially true when chronic anxiety enters the picture.

Lauren, a classic worrier, realized that her anxiety was hurting her marriage. Like others with generalized anxiety disorder, she was frequently overwhelmed by anticipatory anxiety and spent much of her time ruminating on possible catastrophes. She was particularly worried about her only child, Anna. Her most recent worry was about which school would be best for Anna, who was entering kindergarten in the fall. When her sister asked Lauren what Lauren's husband thought about the options, Lauren just shook her head.

"It's always the same with Rob. No matter what I'm worried about, he refuses to even consider my concerns. So many things could go wrong. I've heard that one of the kindergarten teachers at the neighborhood school is really mean. What if Anna gets her as a teacher? If Anna starts off on the wrong foot, she might hate school forever. This could completely color the trajectory of her entire education. But when I say this, Rob just rolls his eyes and says I'm making mountains out of molehills, that Anna is a happy, easygoing little girl and will be fine wherever she goes—period, end of conversation. He won't take anything I say seriously. And then when I keep on him about it, he either gets annoyed or shuts down and refuses to talk with me at all.

"His logical engineer's mind used to be one of the things that I loved and appreciated about him. He's always so calm about everything. Everything with him can be factored into some logical analysis. But now it's driving me crazy; *everything* is just logic to him. Any concern I have is met with this brick wall of reason and tossed aside.

"It feels as if he doesn't care about my thoughts—or *me*—at all. I don't think he even understands where I'm coming from. I used to think my anxiety was the problem, but now I think it's my marriage too. It's as if I don't have a husband anymore—or at least, this isn't what I wanted when I envisioned going through my life with a partner."

We have heard countless clients express frustrations similar to Lauren's. Their pain of not feeling understood and cared for by the one they love becomes a palpable presence in the therapy room. Of course, we all want to be understood, especially by the one we love. Unfortunately, struggles with empathy and support for one another are common in committed relationships. This is particularly the case, however, in relationships in which one partner has an anxiety disorder or heightened anxiety.

In this chapter, you'll gain an understanding of the neuroscience of connection and learn some of the ways connection can be disrupted when one partner has a chronic anxiety disorder. You will also gain a greater understanding of your partner's responses to your anxiety. But first, let's try to get our heads around the brain.

The Neurobiology of Connection

Neurologically, the impasse between you and your partner makes perfect sense. When you are flooded with anxiety and your partner isn't, you and your partner are actually "speaking" from different places in your brains. To understand this, let's look at how the brain works.

The Three-Part Brain

The human brain is composed of many different structures, each of which, like the organs in the rest of your body, performs specific functions and works with the others to ensure your optimal functioning. Although each brain structure is unique, neuroscientists have grouped them into three different "families," or parts, based on their location and the tasks they perform. The three parts that make up our "triune brain" are known by a few different names; in this book we will refer to them as the *hindbrain*, the *midbrain*, and the *forebrain*.

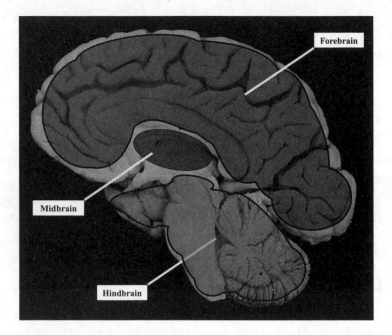

As you can see from the diagram, the hindbrain lies deep within the brain, near where the brain connects with the spinal column. The structures within the hindbrain are largely responsible for controlling bodily functions basic to survival, such as heart rate, breathing, and hunger. The midbrain, as its name suggests, is located approximately in the middle of the brain and is largely responsible for our experience of emotions. The forebrain is located above the hindbrain and midbrain, and is the most recent part of the brain in our evolutionary development. The highly developed forebrain is largely responsible for our ability to think logically and rationally. It is because of our large forebrains that we can engage in complex thought and communicate with written and spoken language.

Anxiety and the Midbrain-Forebrain Disconnect

When you are experiencing anxiety and are flooded with emotion, your midbrain (responsible for emotion) becomes highly activated. Simultaneously, communication between your midbrain and your forebrain (responsible for logic and reason) is interrupted. Rather than allowing the two to work in tandem, your midbrain takes over. Your rational forebrain, which usually steps in with logical appraisals of the situation at hand and helps you see that alarm is not necessary, cannot offer the midbrain its input. Unable to be calmed by reason, you are at the mercy of your emotions. In effect, your midbrain has gone rogue.

Your partner, however, is likely not flooded by anxiety. Thus your partner's midbrain and forebrain are engaged in teamwork: your partner's forebrain logically appraises your fears and informs his midbrain that there's no reason for panic. When you go to your partner for support, he will most likely offer this same logical appraisal to you. *Your* midbrain, however, having gone rogue, isn't communicating with your forebrain and can't even take in your partner's logical input. You and your partner might as well be speaking different languages. In a way, you are: your midbrain is speaking the language of emotion undiluted by your own logic, and your partner's forebrain is speaking the language of logic applied to the emotional midbrain. Because you are speaking different languages, you won't experience satisfying communication or connection. Rather, you're likely to feel emptiness, isolation, and frustration at not being understood. Both you and your partner will feel that your words and needs are lost in translation.

EXERCISE 4.1
Colors of Logic and Emotion

This visualization exercise will enhance your understanding of the brain-based communication barriers we just discussed. Your goal is to understand yourself and your partner without judgment but, instead, with openness, kindness, curiosity, and even receptivity— and from this understanding build a sense of connection, one in which you can honor and even appreciate your differences.

Having the previous diagram of the three-part brain handy will be especially helpful. As with previous exercises, you can read through the following script a few times to familiarize yourself with it and then follow it from memory, record the script and then listen to it as you do the exercise, or have a friend or your therapist read it to you.

Find a comfortable place, where you won't be disturbed for a while. Now take some nice, slow, deep breaths, and as you exhale, think of the word "relax."

And now close your eyes and continue to take slow, deep breaths, thinking of the word "relax" with every exhalation. And as you become more comfortable and relaxed, you may discover that you can easily use your imagination to experience and apply your new knowledge of the three-part brain.

And within this context, perhaps you can elicit a memory of a specific time when you and your partner were at odds with each other—a time when you felt uncomfortable—when you experienced uncomfortable feelings of anxiety, fear, or worry—and even worse, when you and your partner were in serious disconnect as a result—when you were worried, afraid, or upset—and you felt the connection between you and your partner dissolve—and you felt so alone—and maybe very sad. And you felt misunderstood, because your partner just couldn't get away from his or her own point of view and connect to your experience.

Perhaps you can imagine a specific time when the two of you were neither connected nor emotionally attuned—talking but not really communicating.

And as you bring up that memory, where are you? Perhaps you are at home—in your bedroom, in the kitchen—or perhaps you are in the car. Now allow the memory of that exchange to come up—and let yourself really feel the feelings you had on that occasion: the annoyance—the irritation—perhaps the worsening of your anxiety or a feeling of hopelessness. Recall your negative feelings, perhaps the increasing feelings of hostility, hurt, disconnect, and being misunderstood and unsupported. Hold this image, and hold the feelings. And now go back to the words you spoke to each other, or if you don't remember all the words, that's okay. Just imagine what the two of you would typically say. Now freeze this scene in your mind's eye.

Now recall the picture of the three-part brain—so that you can see the brain in your mind's eye. And imagine that you can see directly into your partner's brain, to get a better understanding of the way his or her brain is working. As you view your partner's brain, imagine that you are able to see the three distinct parts: the hindbrain toward the bottom, the midbrain in the middle, and the forebrain at the top.

Now imagine that your partner is speaking from that logical, rational place. Maybe your partner is giving you the typical first response of suggestions—solutions—trying to respond to your anxiety with logic. And as you see your partner speaking to you, remember that he or she is speaking the language of reason—the language of the forebrain. And as this language of reason, the language of the forebrain, is being spoken, allow yourself to see this active part of the brain—the forebrain—light up in *a cool, calm blue, while the other two parts of the brain remain dark and silent.*

Now see the words, too, that are being spoken in the language of the forebrain—this blue language of reason—drift from your partner's mouth to you. And allow yourself to think, There's _____'s blue words, representing the language of reason. What do you imagine your partner is feeling, experiencing, as he or she says these blue words to you?

Now bring your focus back to yourself. And in your mind's eye, picture your own brain. See those three areas: the hindbrain below, the midbrain in the middle, and the forebrain at the top. And bring back the experience of when you felt anxious and disconnected. Remember your anxious feelings—your worries and your fears—your need for your partner to understand you and provide you with support. As you think these thoughts and feel these feelings, imagine your midbrain turning on: lighting up in red—active—flooded with emotion.

As you see yourself speaking to your partner in this language of emotion—the red language of the midbrain—allow yourself to think, This is my emotional brain speaking, speaking the red language of emotion. It's just one part of my brain, but it's the one I'm accessing now. And it makes perfect sense that I am not connecting to my partner, who is speaking the language of reason from the cool, blue center of his or her forebrain. See the two differently colored words meeting but not intermingling—and understand that the reason you and your partner are not connecting is not a lack of care and concern for one another, but because you are speaking two different languages in two different colors that come from two different parts of the brain—cool and hot—blue and red—not intermingling.

Now think to yourself, It's not that my partner doesn't care. It's just that the red doesn't understand the blue, and the blue doesn't understand the red. But I can learn to understand where my partner is coming from and how my red language is affecting my partner. This is the first step in creating connection.

And now, knowing that you can revisit this visualization whenever you believe it would be helpful, take as much time as you need to gradually come back...opening your eyes...feeling alert and calm.

The Brain-to-Brain Connection of Attunement

Attunement, being intellectually and emotionally in sync with one another, is crucial to relationships at every developmental stage. The opposite of isolation, attunement encompasses a sense of relatedness: shared interest, curiosity, and understanding. Attunement is first achieved during infancy through an entirely nonverbal language of emotions. It is a language of shared looks and glances, shared smiles, soothing touch, and sounds of laughter and contentment. In the first year of life, we learn a rich, complex language of connection, even before we learn to speak. It is also a shared language of sorrow or discomfort. Even as we grow older and develop the capacity to communicate through the spoken word, attunement continues to be conveyed largely nonverbally. Words barely scratch the surface when compared to the depth of compassion and care that can be felt through a mutual gaze or through the comforting touch or sympathetic body posture of an attuned other.

When two individuals are in attunement through this complex web of verbal and nonverbal interaction, they are emotionally on the same page. They experience *emotional resonance*: emotionally, they are humming the same tune. This emotional resonance, or connection, is present because various structures within the midbrain, forebrain, and even hindbrain of the attuned individuals are in sync. Thus when you and your partner are in attunement, many emotion-based centers in your midbrains are literally firing in similar patterns in response to one another.

Attunement does not, however, suggest that your emotions are identical. When an infant expresses distress by crying, for example, an attuned caregiver does not become distraught to match the feelings of the baby. The caregiver approaches the infant softly and calmly, recognizing and meeting the baby's needs for comfort and support. In the same way, if you are stressed, you might reach out to your partner for support. Your partner doesn't show support by becoming as stressed as you are. An attuned partner ideally provides you with care and attention to help you to restore an inner sense of well-being.

As we grow older, attunement remains fundamental in our experience of relationships. In love relationships, attunement results in emotional intimacy, where we find a fluency and mutual resonance in the shared language of emotion. Daniel Siegel, a neuroscientist who has extensively studied interpersonal bonds, emotion, and self-regulation, writes of attunement (Siegel 2007, 290): "[S]uch resonant states feel good as we feel 'felt' by another, no longer alone but in connection. This is the heart of empathic relationship, as we sense a clear image of our mind in the mind of another." This resonant connection helps cement our intimate relationships. We gain a sense of fulfillment as we share our joys together, and we, likewise, gain a sense of well-being in times of stress or struggle when an attuned partner is able to sense our needs. In fact, to reach out to another person for comfort in times of fear or stress is a basic human impulse.

Because the experience of attunement with a significant other is powerful, ruptures in attuned connection bring about a sense of absence, loss, and even distress. Yet these ruptures in attunement are inevitable in all relationships, no matter how solid. There are times when you just fall out of sync with one another. It's important, therefore, that you both have the ability to repair ruptures when they occur. Just as quickly as you fall out of sync, with some flexibility you can repair the disconnect and engage one another in attunement again.

Anxiety and Ruptures in Attunement

When you become flooded with anxiety, you lose the emotional flexibility needed to resume attuned connection. Recall from the beginning of chapter 2 that our brains are hardwired in such a way that it's far easier to become flooded by emotion than to manage these emotions with reason. When you become overwhelmed with anxiety, your emotion-based midbrain goes into hyperdrive, and you become more or less cut off from your forebrain's rational, analytical input. You begin to speak the language of pure emotion and are unable to get in sync with your partner, who has more access to her forebrain. When your emotions are revved, it's very hard, without your newly acquired skills from part 1 of this book, to reengage your forebrain, calm your anxious emotions, and regain the attunement and emotional connection. Attunement requires a balance of forebrain and midbrain activity (Siegel 2007). This means that the midbrain needs to be functioning at optimal levels of activation, where you are able to experience emotion without being overtaken by it. This, of course, is not the case when you are flooded with anxiety.

Again, imagine that you are experiencing overpowering feelings of fear and worry, and that you go to your partner for support. Regardless of your partner's response, without a balance of midbrain and forebrain activation, the sense of safety and well-being that accompanies attuned connection will be lacking. Even the most responsive partner will be unable to provide the sense of well-being that your anxiety disorder has taken from you.

In the absence of a sense of comfort through connection, it's easy to feel that your partner isn't "there" for you, to feel angry, and to withdraw even further, widening the gulf that already exists. Your focus narrows to your own thoughts, body responses, and decisions, and then to your increased isolation. In the face of these overwhelming stressors, it's understandable that you would withdraw. This inner focus can lead you to lose sight of your partner's feelings and thus fall farther away from the sense of connection that you desire.

Now that you have learned the anxiety-regulating techniques presented in part 1, you are equipped to begin to bridge the gulf that may have developed between you and your partner. You can now reestablish the midbrain-forebrain communication that opens the way for the attuned connection that was lost when you were flooded by anxiety. Now you can broaden the focus of your recovery to include your interactions with your partner and change them for the better. The first step in this process is to gain an understanding of your partner's responses and reactions to your anxiety. Once you develop a broader understanding of these reactions and responses, you will be better able to empathize with your partner *and* alter your communication patterns.

Understanding Your Partner's Reactions to Your Anxiety

The most effective way to better understand your partner's reactions to your anxiety—the goal of this section—is to temporarily shift your attention from yourself to your partner's inner experience. Throughout our years of clinical practice, we have found that partners' reactions typically take one or some combination of three modes: the *appeal*, the *attack*, and the *retreat*. Each person is different, but you are likely to find your partner in the following descriptions.

The Appeal: Speaking the Language of Reason

Most commonly, partners first react to your anxiety by trying to help you see that your fears are illogical. Recall that when you are flooded with anxiety, your partner is much more in touch with the logical forebrain than you are. So your partner's first impulse may be to appeal to your sense of reason. Partners often think that with logic, you'll snap out of it and feel better. But as you have learned, rational arguments are not powerful enough to defuse your anxiety.

Put yourself in your partner's shoes. Imagine that your typical roles are reversed: your partner is overwhelmed with anxiety and has come to you for help and support. You don't want your partner to suffer. Assuming that you're not overwhelmed with emotion yourself, you will most likely offer a suggestion based on a logical appraisal of the situation. But your well-intended support doesn't even put a dent in your partner's anxiety. It's understandable that you feel frustrated with yourself for being unable to help, with your partner for not benefiting from your well-intended advice, and with the fact that you live with someone who is chronically anxious.

Continue to imagine yourself in your partner's shoes. Your frustration may also intensify when you try to reestablish an attuned connection with your anxious partner. Indeed, reestablishing this connection probably feels more urgent because your partner is in a great deal of distress. But this effort to connect won't succeed, because the communication between your partner's midbrain and forebrain has been interrupted by your partner's intense emotions. The result is that you don't feel any attuned connection with your anxious partner. You feel isolated—alone. What's more, you feel that all your well-intentioned efforts at connection have failed.

Now step back into your own shoes and remember your own repeated experiences of isolation, when you have been flooded with anxiety and discouraged that your partner couldn't connect with you. At those moments, your partner may have been trying to establish the very connection you desired. And your partner may have felt frustration and a similar sense of isolation when the connection wasn't made. All of this mounting frustration and failure to connect can sometimes set the stage for a shift into the attack or the retreat.

The Attack: Reacting Emotionally

Frustrated by his inability to calm you down and reestablish connection, your partner may become emotional. Reason may be replaced with anger, disappointment, or even rage. Harsh words and blame are common in this mode of reacting. Your partner might say that you should be able to deal with your anxiety on your own, that you are too dependent, or that he is tired of constantly having to deal with your anxiety. You might feel as if your partner is belittling you for anxiety that you can't control. Past and ongoing disputes between you might enter the argument here, adding fuel to the fire.

When your partner is on the attack, neither of you is calm or in a frame of mind to give or receive support. Your interaction is intense, but it won't foster mutual connection. Rather, it fosters increasing isolation and hurt.

The Retreat: Sensing Defeat and Seeking Isolation

In sharp contrast to the attack, the retreat mode is marked by a *lack* of interaction. Your partner may retreat emotionally or physically, or both, in an effort to get away from the conflict or your anxiety. While the retreat may feel like the calm after the storm (especially if it follows the attack), the isolation and loss of connection you both experience can be just as devastating as the more active conflict of the attack.

You may feel as if your partner, in retreat mode, is light-years away. Even if you are in the same room, the distance between you couldn't seem greater. Whether your partner holds a tight-lipped silence that stems from anger or goes emotionally numb and fails to connect, the retreat creates a stalemate. The silence can be just as hurtful and harmful as a heated exchange if the climate of disconnect between the two of you is allowed to linger.

While it's common to shift from one mode of reacting to the next sequentially, everyone is different and responds to her partner's intense anxiety differently. An awareness of the three types of reactions provides you with a better understanding of your partner's responses to your anxiety. It allows you to begin to step back from your own inner experience to gain a broader appreciation of the rifts in connection between you and your partner. There are many ways to reinforce your newfound larger perspective on the disconnect you often feel with your partner. Especially effective is the following journal exercise, which will help you further cultivate this ability.

EXERCISE 4.2
See Your Partner's Perspective

Writing in a journal about your partner's reactions can help you appreciate your differences, appreciate your partner as separate from you, and learn to accept that separateness. Although your partner may act and react very differently than you do, he may be suffering, too. Ironically, accepting your partner's separateness without judgment may be the first step in re-creating intimate connection.

In this exercise you will write in a journal about:

- The ways that your anxiety has affected your partner

- Your partner's typical responses to your anxiety

- What makes sense about those responses

- What you appreciate about your partner

You will need four sheets of paper and a favorite pen, or if you are comfortable using a computer, open four new documents or one document with four separate pages. The physical act of writing or typing will help you process your thoughts differently than you do when you just think about them. Furthermore, when your thoughts are written down, you can return to them at any time and gain new insights or new emotional distance. Keep these pages handy, because you will be asked to return to them again in exercise 6.1.

When you have assembled your writing utensils, turn off the phone ringer and find a comfortable place where you won't be disturbed. Center yourself by taking four slow, deep breaths (see chapter 2 for breathing techniques if you need a quick refresher). When you feel quiet, title the four pages as follows and write your responses without any concern about how they sound:

Page 1: *Ways my anxiety has affected* _____ [your partner's name]

Page 2: _____'s [your partner's name] *typical responses to my anxiety*

Page 3: *Ways that* _____'s [your partner's name] *responses to my anxiety make sense, considering my partner's perspective*

For this topic, you might consider how the following characteristics might help explain those responses:

- your partner's family background

- modeling

- gender

- temperament

- education or occupational training

Page 4: *What I appreciate about* _____ [your partner's name]

- *Character:* Morals, ethics at your partner's core (honest, trustworthy, hardworking, and so on)

- *Behavior:* Ways your partner supports you or the household, ways your partner makes your life easier

- *Endearing traits*

Wrapping It Up

When you pay attention to your partner's internal experience during your interactions, you inevitably soften your heart to her. This may be difficult at first, but the reward will be well worth your effort. As you begin to gain an appreciation of your partner's experience, you pave the way to restored connection and deeper understanding of one another. In the next chapters, you will walk farther down this path, learning to validate and empathize with your partner.

chapter 5

Changing How You Handle Conflict

"This really isn't the end of the world, Michelle." Tim's voice had the strained, high-pitched tone of caring turned to exasperation. "The microwave is fully functional, and we can't afford to go out to dinner every night while the kitchen gets repaired. It's just a burst pipe; you make it sound like the house is falling down around us. We can eat off paper plates while the kitchen sink's getting fixed, and for the thousandth time there's *no* significant risk of bacteria forming where the kitchen flooded." It had been two days since the pipe under the kitchen sink had burst, and it would be five days until the kitchen would be back in working order again. But Tim and Michelle were beginning to fear that it would take longer to repair the rupture that seemed to be widening between them.

"I don't understand how you can be so insensitive!" Michelle was near tears. "You know that I have OCD. You even read that book on it that my therapist recommended. You must know by now that if something is worrying me, I can't just put it out of my mind like you can. I *can't* stop thinking about how contaminated every-thing is. The workmen are leaving empty soda cans and fast-food wrappers in the kitchen where they're working, which, of course, attracts ants and cockroaches—maybe even rats. Am I the only one who cares about the children getting sick?" Michelle started to cry. "I'm already up to my eyeballs in stress, and now you're laying into me, too. I need you to be on my side, but you're on the firing squad instead."

"I'm not about to sit here and pretend that what you're saying is reasonable, Michelle," Tim volleyed back, as he walked out of the room. "If you're waiting for me to agree with you, you're going to be waiting a long time, because I just don't."

"Look, I have to take a time-out right now. I'm going to the bedroom." Michelle disappeared down the hall.

If you suffer from high anxiety, there's a good chance that you and your partner will react quite differently to various bumps in the road, just as Michelle and Tim had different reactions to the burst pipe in their kitchen. As we discussed in chapter 4, these differing reactions can give rise to ruptures in your sense of connection and partnership. When Tim was unable to corroborate Michelle's fears and perceptions, she responded by going on the attack, essentially giving him the message that he was an insensitive, inadequate partner. Tim shot back that Michelle, not he, was the one being unreasonable—getting in one last volley before walking out of the room and initiating the retreat. At this point, Michelle recognized that she was getting triggered, so she took a time-out, halting the destructive escalation of conflict between her and her partner.

Although it was said in a flurry of anger, Tim's final comment hit on a crucial truth, something that no amount of stress reduction on Michelle's part could change: he did not share her perspective. When you have anxiety and your partner does not, your viewpoints will often diverge. This divergence can give rise to conflicts that may worsen your anxiety or trigger other intense emotions, such as anger and hurt, as it did for Michelle. Yet how do you interact with your partner when conflict arises, without falling into familiar yet destructive communication patterns such as the attack and the retreat? Your divergent viewpoints will remain a source of rupture unless you allow room for both viewpoints to coexist. In this chapter you will gain the ability to honor your own feelings, fears, and perspectives, while simultaneously acknowledging and honoring those of your partner. This ability will make all the difference in shifting from *reacting* to *intentionally responding* to your partner, thereby helping you remain in connection with one another as you explore your differences.

Reactions vs. Intentional Responses

What is the difference between reacting and intentionally responding? As we see it, *reactions* are rash, intense responses to your partner. If you're in a reactive mode and you come into conflict with your partner, emotion—intense emotion, at that—will dictate your actions and words. It's not just anxiety that can get in your way. Anger, frustration, disappointment, and sadness, to name just a few emotions, can become just as overwhelming and destructive as your unchecked anxiety has been. This is because these emotions, even in the absence of anxiety, can lead to emotional flooding.

This emotional flooding will send your midbrain into hyperdrive. Just as when you become flooded with anxiety, the communication between your midbrain and your logic-based forebrain is impeded. Your emotions blast with the intensity of a megaphone, while your more-rational appraisals of your partner and your situation barely have the attention getting power of a whisper. Emotions escalate, conflict intensifies, and you find yourself embroiled in either the attack or the retreat with your partner, simply because reactions, whether they are fueled by fear or another emotion, have run amok. A sense of connection and partnership is again lost.

Intentional responses, on the other hand, are not governed by a tidal wave of unrestrained emotion. When you're *intentionally responding* to your partner, both the emotional and cognitive systems of your brain are online and communicating fluently with one another. When both you and your partner are able to access this emotionally grounded and neurologically balanced state during a conflict, interpersonal communication can flow freely. This is because you're able to let both emotion and rational thought inform your actions and your responses to your partner. As a result, you and your partner can experience a sense of connection and attunement—even in the face of conflict. No longer embroiled in the uncontained reactions of attack and retreat, you have the mental and emotional flexibility to value both your and your partner's differing perspectives.

Moving from Reacting to Intentionally Responding

The first step in moving from reacting to intentionally responding is to *interrupt* your reactions. When you notice yourself slipping into a reactive mode, you can use a time-out to interrupt the reaction and de-escalate your emotional flooding. After the time-out, when you've regained your sense of calm, you can respond first to your needs and then to the needs of your partner. With the tools provided in this chapter, you will learn to identify your unmet needs during conflict with your partner. Next, you will acknowledge the vulnerable feelings that the conflict elicited and begin to nurture yourself and ease your distress. Finally, you then will apply the communication skills of *mirroring* and *validation*, taught later, to engage your partner powerfully and effectively. In so doing, you will transform your experience of conflict. If your partner is learning the mirroring and validation tools as well, you will have more of a common ground to start from. However, even if your partner is not familiar with these tools, your relationship will still benefit greatly by your employing them.

Putting Conflict on Hold with a Time-Out

Anxiety can not only bring about fear, panic, and nervousness, but also lead to conflict in your relationship, as was the case with Tim and Michelle. At this point in the game, you're already skilled at identifying the cognitive, emotional, and physical indicators of your anxiety. You're also well practiced at taking a time-out when these red flags arise and returning to a state of equilibrium with your time-out techniques. Now you can begin applying the time-outs to de-escalate your emotional reactivity during interactions with your partner.

EXERCISE 5.1
Take a Time-Out When You Are Emotionally Triggered

When you notice the following red-flag emotions intensifying during interactions with your partner, it's time for a time-out.

Anger	Impatience	Overwhelm
Despair	Inadequacy	Panic
Exhaustion	Irritability	Resentment
Failure	Isolation	Sadness
Fear	Loneliness	Shame
Frustration	Nervousness	

111

Once you've completed your time-out exercises, communication between your forebrain and midbrain will be reestablished. You'll be able to calmly evaluate the emotions that set you off, then take the next step: giving yourself the emotional reassurance you need. The next exercise teaches you how to do just that.

Identifying Your Unmet Needs and Meeting Them

Regardless of the specifics of your conflict with your partner—what he said or didn't say, did or didn't do—your hurt or anger, when you get to its root, stems from your desire for connection with your partner. And that desire wasn't met. Missing were the qualities of connection: gentleness, attentiveness, care, a sense of partnership, and the reassuring feeling that you're not alone in your distress.

Those with whom we're most intimately connected have the power to hurt us the most. The emotional connection we experience with our partners is so powerful that its absence is profoundly painful. More often than not, we don't recognize that it's this loss of connection that causes us to react with criticism, defensiveness, contempt, or stonewalling—behaviors that relationship expert John Gottman (1994) calls the "Four Horsemen of the Apocalypse" of a partnership. Now that you know that a loss of connection lies behind your intense reactions to your partner's words or behavior, you can identify the specific trigger that ruptured the connection.

Although the loss of connection is painfully palpable, you will discover, through the following exercise, that you can be okay even though the needs that you want your partner to fulfill aren't met all the time. This is empowering. In reality, no one is able to meet all of your needs all of the time. The good news from this realization is that you aren't completely dependent on others for your soothing and validation. You can give yourself the gift of self-compassion, self-soothing, and self-understanding. While receiving care from your partner is an essential component of any good relationship, self-care is essential as well. You can provide yourself with some of the comfort, care, and emotional support that you yearn for.

EXERCISE 5.2
Identify and Meet Your Emotional Needs

In this exercise you will first identify your emotional needs and then learn how you yourself can meet those needs, when necessary, with acceptance, compassion, and self-validation.

After you have calmed yourself with your stress-reducing techniques, and before you end your time-out, take the following steps:

1. Remember what your partner did or said during your last interaction that triggered your reaction.

2. Shift your focus from the conflict itself to the feelings it stirred in you. You can refer back to the list of emotional triggers in the previous exercise to help you identify the emotions that arose for you.

3. Now that you've identified your *feelings,* reflect on and identify the underlying need or longing that your partner didn't meet. You can use the following list to spur your thinking.

comfort	feeling needed	feeling valued
companionship	feeling respected	feeling worthy
feeling attractive	feeling unburdened	partnership
feeling desired		safety
feeling heard	feeling understood	support
feeling important		

4. Now that you've identified your unmet needs during that interaction, take a moment to *give yourself* the particular support that you were yearning for. To do so, get in touch with that wise-parent part of yourself that you learned to access in exercise 3.3. To get in touch with this wise-parent self, think back to times when you've shown that care and concern for others. The wise parent is that strong, nurturing part of yourself that is receptive, caring, and supportive—not judging, shaming, or criticizing. Now imagine showing that same care and concern for yourself that you've shown for others.

5. Think of a statement that you would have liked to hear from your partner: the caring, loving response to your distress that you wanted but didn't get. If you like, get a pen and some paper, and write the words down.

6. Imagine the vulnerable part of you standing in front of you. With the loving, affirming voice of your wise-parent self, silently repeat the statement that you yearned to hear.

7. Cross your arms and embrace yourself, allowing the wise parent to comfort the part of you that feels vulnerable and in need. Give yourself this comfort for as long as you wish.

8. When you've given yourself sufficient comfort and validation, take a deep breath, put your thumb and forefinger together making an "okay" symbol with your hand, and say to yourself, *I'm okay.* By doing this you are creating a cue that will automatically re-elicit the comfort and support of your wise-parent self. And know that at any time during your interactions with your partner, you can put your thumb and forefinger together and use this cue to remind yourself that you're okay. And because you are okay, you can be in control of your reactions. In this way you can always provide yourself the care, comfort, and self-support that you need.

9. Bring your time-out to a close, knowing that just because your time-out is ending, your self-care doesn't need to stop. With the knowledge that you have a multitude of self-care tools at your fingertips, you can now return from your time-out and check in with your partner.

Initiating Dialogue with Your Partner

Now that you are calm and have given yourself validation, you're in an optimal state of mind to communicate with your partner. Your baseline stress level is back in the green zone, you're emotionally on firmer ground, and you can be intentionally responsive rather than reactive in conversation. Because you have already provided yourself with some of the comfort and understanding that you wanted from your partner, you're less likely to become emotionally flooded again when discussing this need with your partner, as you'll learn how to do next.

By approaching your partner now, you have the opportunity to repair any ruptures that occurred before your time-out. The first step in the repair process is asking your partner if it's a good time to talk. Unlike you, your partner hasn't necessarily just had a time-out for self-soothing, so you want to ensure that your partner is in an open, responsive frame of mind when you resume your dialogue.

If your partner doesn't feel that it's a good time to talk, decide on a time during the next twenty-four hours, if possible, when you will sit down together to continue your interaction. When you do resume the conversation, make sure that you both are in a calm state. It's important that neither of you is too stressed, tired, or distracted to give the other your attention.

EXERCISE 5.3
Constructively Communicate
Your Needs

When you and your partner do feel that it's a good time to talk, initiate dialogue following these three steps:

1. Start with the positive, stating what you appreciate about your partner.

2. Share the feeling you identified as painful, your partner's action that led to the feelings, and the deeper feeling of vulnerability in you that it elicited. Use the following strategies for constructive communication:

    a. Use "I" statements. Express your feelings and experiences using the pronoun "I." For example, "I felt frustrated when you told me there's nothing to worry about. When you said that, I felt so alone," "I felt disconnected when you refused to spend any more time discussing my concern and you just turned back to your computer. I felt so unimportant to you," or "I felt shame when you said I was overreacting. When you said that, I wanted to just disappear."

    b. Focus on your own feelings; don't make assumptions regarding your partner's thoughts or intentions, as in, "I know you think I'm overreacting," or "I know you think I'm a hypochondriac." Instead, stick to what you were feeling, as in, "I want you to understand how scared I get when…"

    c. Keep it short and sweet. This dialogue works better if you are succinct in your communication. Your partner is more likely to receive your message if you use only a couple of sentences. Too much information makes it hard for your partner to take in and remember what you said.

3. Ask for your partner's feedback and response to what you've just shared by saying something like, "I'm open to your feedback and response to what I've just shared with you." After listening to your partner's response, use the mirroring and validation tools taught next. Throughout this conversation with your partner, remember that you are using new dialogue skills that your partner may lack. Nevertheless, you may be pleased to discover how much the tone of your interaction changes when you bring effective communication skills to the table.

Developing Active Listening Skills: Mirroring

Couples therapy experts and authors Harville Hendrix and Helen Hunt (1994) have said that the first requirement of love is listening. Unfortunately, most of us have not developed very good listening skills. We get too caught up in our own thoughts, feelings, and responses to hear accurately what our partners are saying to us. We often place too much focus on ourselves and, in doing so, fail to really hear the other. When this occurs, we fall prey to what we call the "three I's of miscommunication": inattention, interrupting, and interjecting.

Inattention

When you are listening to another person, it's natural to be distracted by the running commentary in your own head. While your partner is talking, you probably find yourself thinking about what you want to say next or reflecting on your opinion of what your partner is saying. You are busy evaluating and judging your partner's point of view. This is not conducive to building a sense of connection and to promoting mutual understanding in your relationship. When you listen to your own internal running commentary, you don't actually hear what your partner is saying. Or you might hear some of it but miss some crucial points. This inattention, more often than not, leads to misinterpretation. Making matters worse, you may often react to those misinterpretations, becoming emotionally triggered by what you *think* your partner is telling you without checking to make sure that your interpretation is correct.

Interrupting and Interjecting

Interruption and interjection go hand in hand. Whether you wait until your partner stops talking or cut in midsentence, you are interrupting by immediately interjecting your own thoughts, feelings, and opinions. When you interrupt your partner, you're not giving her the time and space to be fully heard. This is counter to the goal of openness and receptivity. Whether you're jumping to conclusions, misinterpreting your partner's words, changing the subject, or trying to piggyback on what you *believe* your partner is expressing, you're not considering and valuing your partner's opinion. The connection you seek to establish through the dialogue can be destroyed in this way.

While your partner is speaking, there may be times when you feel anxious that you won't have a chance to express your opinion. This is a common feeling, especially when you first begin practicing the mirroring technique. When these fears arise, know that you, too, will have a turn to speak. Expressing your own response to your partner is just as important as actively listening to her viewpoint, but if you skip over the listening stage, immediately thinking about and expressing your own response, you're denying your partner the very experience of being heard that you yourself crave.

EXERCISE 5.4
Mirroring

Two crucial components of the process of communication are giving your partner a chance to communicate what he needs to say and checking to make sure that you have understood what your partner said. This is what's done in *mirroring*. You listen attentively to your partner and then "reflect" this communication by restating what you believe your partner has said to you. Finally, you check to see if you "got it right," giving your partner a chance to clarify anything you might have missed and confirming what you correctly understood. If you bypass these three fundamental steps, you increase the likelihood of miscommunication, heightened emotional activation, and renewed conflict. Learning and applying the following three steps of mirroring is a simple, concrete way to avoid falling prey to the three "I's" of miscommunication.

Step 1: Listen to your partner. While your partner is speaking, don't divert your attention by thinking about:

- How you're going to respond

- How what your partner is saying is wrong

- How your opinion is right

Instead, cultivate an attitude of curiosity:

- Welcome what your partner shares with you.

- Appreciate the novelty and uniqueness of your partner's perspective, just as you would appreciate the novelty of exploring a foreign culture.

- If you notice that your stress is on the rise, take a few deep breaths or initiate some four-square breathing as you continue to listen. Doing some calming breath work can help you maintain the attitude of openness and curiosity you are working to cultivate.

Actively placing all of your attention on simply taking in what your partner is saying can be frustrating if you think your partner has the facts all wrong. Just remember, correcting facts is not the goal. The goal is to offer careful attention and precise listening to your partner as she attempts to communicate with you.

Step 2: Reflect. When your partner finishes speaking, begin your response by saying, "Let me see if I understood everything you just said. You said that..." Then repeat back what your partner just communicated to you as close to verbatim as you can. You probably won't get it perfect, but try to get the gist of what you heard your partner say. In reflecting your partner's words calmly and caringly, you convey that you are making an earnest effort to listen.

Step 3: Do a content check. When you've repeated what you think your partner said, ask, "Did I get that right?"

Good communication is not about proving who is right, but about making the effort to really hear one another. Mirroring shows your partner that you are making that effort, that you listened closely to what she said and want to understand it—even if you disagree. Once you have done this, you're ready for the next step of constructive communication: *validating* your partner's point of view and experience.

Validating Your Partner

It's only human to wish that your partner always agreed with you, saw the world just as you see it, and shared your opinions, feelings, and convictions. But this just doesn't happen. While the uniqueness of every person can lend variety and excitement to relationships, it can also be a source of contention, frustration, and disconnect. You and your partner will sometimes disagree or have trouble even understanding your differences. By validating your partner following his communication, you acknowledge that his thoughts and feelings make sense, given his perspective. This doesn't mean that you necessarily agree with your partner's perspective, but that you can look at it from your partner's viewpoint and validate it. You give equal value to the different points of view that you and your partner hold.

According to psychologist Alan Fruzzetti (2006), validation conveys understanding and acceptance of your partner. By validating your partner's point of view, you are acknowledging and honoring your different viewpoints. The key to mastering validation is to embrace the reality that you can validate another person's thoughts and feelings *even if* your opinions are in direct opposition to them. This is why validating your partner can be challenging. Recognizing that your partner has very different opinions, reactions, emotions, and interests than you do can cause anxiety. You may be afraid that it means you're wrong (when you *know* you aren't) or that the two of you won't be able to stay together. On the contrary, for your relationship to work, you both need to accept that you are unique, separate individuals and give each other the space to express your individuality. Validation offers you a way to honor this essential separateness by acknowledging that two opposing viewpoints can coexist: one needn't invalidate the other.

It can also be especially difficult to practice validation because, since you suffer from anxiety, you're probably emotionally exhausted. You may just want reassurance from your partner and feel unable to offer validation to him. The act of listening to and validating your partner, however, can lessen your anxiety by shifting your focus outside of yourself. This is an important step in mastering your anxiety. Happily, at the same time it does wonders for your relationship.

EXERCISE 5.5
Validation

The mechanics of validation are simple:

1. After you've summarized your partner's statements and your partner has confirmed that you heard them accurately (the final step in mirroring), validate your partner by saying:

    "It makes perfect sense that you think, feel, or are experiencing _____ [restate what your partner has expressed]."

    "It makes sense because, from your point of view, _____ [say what you believe supports your partner's reasoning]."

    This lets your partner know that her perspective makes sense to you in view of her way of thinking, past experiences, temperament, anxiety levels, and so on. It acknowledges and validates her feelings and thoughts without requiring you to claim that you agree with them. Your validation of your partner is a profound gift to both your partner and yourself. Feeling understood is soothing and diminishes anger. It also prevents the escalation of conflict. Furthermore, as you validate your partner, you model the very behavior that you yearn to receive from her in return.

2. Take responsibility for what you might have done, intentionally or unintentionally, that upset your partner by saying:

    "And your feelings make sense, in view of _____ [list your actions or words that your partner found upsetting]."

The ability to take ownership of your actions in this way is a crucial skill for you to develop in order to reduce conflict in any relationship.

Using Mini Time-Outs to Enhance Your Interaction

Even if you become a master communicator, skilled at mirroring and validating, it's still easy to become triggered, especially if your partner doesn't respond as you would like. If you feel that familiar reactivity rearing its ugly head and your stress level rising, recognize that you are at risk of moving away from that calm internal state that promotes optimal communication and interaction with your partner. Of course, you can always take a formal time-out, telling your partner that you need to do so. However, sometimes just a "mini" time-out with a quick relaxation technique or your okay signal from exercise 5.2 is all you need to quickly get your stress back in the green zone.

You can use the closed eye roll (exercise 2.3) and four-square breathing (exercise 2.5) while you're in the middle of an interaction with your partner, as described previously. The closed eye roll is perfect for those moments when the dialogue has paused and it's your turn to respond. It allows you to give your nervous system a quick reboot before you continue the conversation. Of course, you wouldn't do this while your partner is speaking, because it would be perceived as a gesture of dismissal. For those times when you can't break eye contact, you can quietly engage in four-square breathing without taking your attention off your partner's words. In this way, you recalibrate your nervous system while simultaneously attending to your partner. With the closed eye roll and four-square breathing, you can remain on track with effective, nonreactive communication, sufficiently regulating your baseline levels of anxiety so that you don't get to the point where a formal time-out is needed. Employing these mini time-outs can do wonders to help lessen reactivity and enhance intentional responses.

Wrapping It Up

All couples experience conflict. If you're in a committed relationship, it's a given. In this sense, the existence of conflict is not a problem. It's how you handle conflict that can make or break a relationship. Negotiating conflict can enhance trust, a sense of partnership, and intimacy. Or it can dismantle every scrap of trust and loving connection that you and your partner once shared. Using the tools that help you negotiate conflict in an intentionally responsive state can make all the difference in the outcome.

By taking a time-out, identifying your own needs, and self-validating, you defuse the powerful emotions that fuel destructive conflict. When you resume communication with your partner from this calm, intentionally responsive state, you're less likely to trigger one another, so that you don't become emotionally flooded and lose attuned connection time and time again. By voicing your needs constructively, mirroring and validating your partner's experience, and using quick self-soothing techniques to promote intentional dialogue, your interactions with your partner will progress down a smoother path.

chapter 6

Increasing Compassion, Empathy, and Connection

The conflict between Michelle and Tim over the burst pipe in their kitchen illustrates the very different reactions to everyday situations that you and your nonanxious partner probably have. Now that you have learned to de-escalate your anxiety with the daily relaxation regimen and time-outs, you have more control over your anxiety. However, the different reactions of you and your partner to events, at times, will continue to cause ruptures in your sense of connection and partnership. When this occurs, feelings of compassion, empathy, and love toward your partner can vaporize in the heat of the moment.

When you and your partner are locked in conflict, each with a different perspective on a given situation, it's easy to get upset by the other's apparent refusal to yield to your point of view. Anger, hurt, sadness, frustration, a sense of alienation—all the various "unpleasant" feelings that arise during conflict—mount with each passing moment of disconnect. As difficult as it may seem during relational rupture, it's essential that you learn to access the very feelings that have apparently vanished: compassion, empathy, and love. These feelings are at the heart of the sense of connection that is the essence of a healthy relationship. It is vital, therefore, to hold on to mutual respect and caring even in the midst of conflict. In this chapter, you will learn how to do this through exercises that help you develop and express feelings of compassion and empathy toward your partner when you are upset.

The Power of Connection

Intimate relationships are innately rewarding. In fact, neuroscience research shows that certain areas of the brain light up in a unique pattern when a person looks at pictures of his romantic partner. This unique—and highly satisfying—activation of the brain helps explain why humans form and maintain romantic attachments.

What makes this experience satisfying is the release of two hormones, *oxytocin* and *vasopressin*, which are largely responsible for the unique pattern of brain activation that sustains romantic attachment. The release of oxytocin and vasopressin promotes a strong sense of emotional connection with the one you love, along with the comfort and security those feelings bring. The release of oxytocin, specifically, is also associated with decreased fear and anxiety. In some instances, it can even help inhibit the brain's release of stress hormones, such as cortisol. Accordingly, the rewards of intentionally engaging in loving thoughts and feelings for your partner are twofold: you're activating your natural drive for romantic connection and reducing your anxiety.

In the following exercise, you will learn how to turn on feelings of love and compassion at will. Just as you learned in chapter 3 to create your own cue to help you return to your safe place, you will learn to create a cue to activate the brain circuitry of the unique romantic bond in order to elicit compassion and love *while* you are experiencing conflict with your partner.

EXERCISE 6.1
Activate Feelings of Love, Care, and Connection

In exercise 4.2 you wrote down the qualities and behaviors you appreciate about your partner. For this exercise, read your previous journal entry over a few times, and if any additional positive or endearing qualities of your partner come to mind, go ahead and add them to your list. Begin this exercise by reading that list a few times. If additional positive qualities of your partner come to mind, go ahead and add them to your list now. Next, either record the following script or have a friend agree to read it to you. When you've made these preparations, find a quiet, comfortable place where you won't be disturbed. Then do a closed eye roll (exercise 2.3) and some four-square breathing (exercise 2.5), setting the foundation for the following visualization.

> *Now that you are settled and relaxed, take some time to enjoy what you most love about your partner—those unique personal attributes that are precious to you— bringing to mind those characteristics, those actions, those aspects of your partner's personality that you appreciate— that you admire or even find wonderful. And as you allow each of these attributes to come to mind, visualize an image of your partner. Maybe it's a still image— your favorite picture—or maybe it's more like a movie clip—helping you look on with a sense of warmth, care, and deep contentment, as you see your partner actively embodying those characteristics that you enjoy most.*
>
> *And as you view this image of your partner in whatever form it may take, notice any sensations that arise in your body. Do you feel relaxed? Is there warmth in your hands or in your stomach? Perhaps you can notice a hint of a smile on your face. And if there is no smile, perhaps you can create one—gently allowing the corners of your*

mouth to curl upward—as you enjoy all the endearing qualities of the one you love—allowing your lips to naturally smile with each exhalation.

And to make it easier for you to elicit these feelings of warmth and care that you are sensing so powerfully right now, you can create a cue that will automatically give rise to these feelings at any time. To create this cue so that your mind and body activate these feelings of love, raise your right hand to your chest, gently placing the open palm of your right hand over your heart. And as you rest your open palm over the place where your heart resides, sense the subtle, steady warmth that begins to emanate from your core collecting in your open hand. And as you feel this warmth gather in the palm of your hand, call forth an image of your partner, an image that elicits all those endearing qualities that you appreciate. And hold this image for a minute or two, as you hold your hand to your heart, enjoying the calm contentment that this sense of compassion brings.

By anchoring this sensation of your hand on your heart, this image, and the accompanying feelings of care and compassion toward your partner, you are training your brain to very quickly push the replay button—so that these good feelings will come back automatically—automatically and quickly. So with this sensation of your hand over your heart, your cue, it will be very easy for you to elicit these soothing, calming, loving feelings of care, compassion, and regard. And you can gain a sense of relief in knowing that you can experience these feelings of compassion at any time you wish, no matter what your partner is or isn't doing—returning these soothing benefits to you by bringing your right hand to your heart and tapping into this warm, soothing sense of care. And when you feel ready to bring this exercise to a close, count slowly from one to twenty, taking all the time you need to open your eyes.

Allowing Opposing Feelings to Coexist

"When I'm upset with Tim, he might as well be Napoleon—or Scrooge," Michelle told her coworker on day five of the kitchen repairs. "I can fill in whatever villain I please, depending on what he's just done that has upset me. The negative is all I see, and anger or hurt is all I feel. It's as if all the good about him—all the reasons I love him and love to be with him—disappear for the moment. I just see the part of him that I'm unhappy with. And I feel abandoned by the husband whose love and care I didn't get."

When you only see the negative about your partner, you've lost sight of the whole picture. You're also slipping into a reactive rather than responsive state, further escalating the sense of conflict between you. And, of course, the escalation of conflict itself will worsen your anxiety.

The following exercise will help you embrace the whole picture of your partner: both the negative and positive feelings that you experience in response to your partner. This gives you the opportunity to welcome both negative and positive feelings that are inevitable when you connect with another human being. You will be able to witness the two sets of feelings almost concurrently. In this way you can acknowledge the negative feelings without getting lost in them.

EXERCISE 6.2
Juxtapose Two Feelings

To prepare for this exercise, familiarize yourself with the following script, record it, or ask a friend or therapist to read it to you. Then go to a quiet place where you won't be disturbed and begin.

Let's start with the negative thoughts and feelings. Take a moment to think about your partner. Think about a particular time when you and your partner were in conflict. Let any feelings of hurt, aloneness, and disappointment come up. And notice whatever thoughts accompany these feelings; for example, He isn't as patient anymore, She might leave me, How can he be so cold to me when I am so good to him? How can he be so oblivious? Why is she so selfish and uncaring? I've told him a thousand times about my anxiety; how can he not get it after living with me for so long!

Now hold on to those upsetting feelings and thoughts; really let them come up for you in all their intensity. And as you do, open your left hand. Now imagine that you are placing all of that negativity into your left hand. Envision all this negativity flowing from your mind into your left palm. And now close your fingers to make a fist, encapsulating all these negative feelings in your fist.

Now, still holding those feelings in your left fist, deliberately shift your attention to positive thoughts and feelings about your partner—taking a few deep breaths— and allowing yourself to become just a little calmer with each exhalation. Now take a moment to slowly bring your right hand to your heart, resting your open palm on your chest, just over the place where your heart beats underneath—your cue to easily elicit the many endearing qualities your partner has—all of the caring, warm, and loving feelings that you feel for your partner. And let those warm, tender feelings and the accompanying thoughts come up—in all their intensity. And now, imagine all of these good feelings flowing directly from your heart into the palm of your open right hand. Feel them gathering in the palm of your hand—and hold them there, cupping your hand into a fist.

And now that you are clasping all of these good feelings in your right fist and all the negative feelings in your left, slowly bring your hands together, interlocking your fingers so that your palms touch—allowing the good feelings to exist alongside the bad—sensing the two sets of feelings coexisting in the same small space. Notice how one set of feelings doesn't cancel out the other. Perhaps you can now be receptive to the difficult parts as well as the good parts that are inevitable in any relationship— receptive to the difficult feelings as well as the good—and acknowledge that at any given time, no matter how all- encompassing your negative feelings toward your partner may seem, you actually have more than that one feeling available to you. You actually have the positive feelings available at the same time. And when you feel ready to bring this exercise to a close, count slowly from one to twenty, taking all the time you need to open your eyes.

Accessing Empathy

In exercises 5.4 and 5.5, you learned how to honor your partner's perspective when it differs from yours by mirroring and validating. Now you can enhance your ability to navigate conflict by increasing your empathy toward your partner's emotional experience. Empathy is the ability to identify with another's feelings and to emotionally put yourself in somebody else's shoes. While you can never experience exactly what another person is feeling, you *can* emotionally tap into the experience of another. When you empathize, you gain a sense of the emotional terrain of another's world, and you convey this understanding to your partner. Couples therapy experts Harville Hendrix and Helen Hunt (1994, 96) state in their book *The Couples Companion,* "Empathy is in many ways like the music that quivers between the separate strings of the lute. It brings us together in a shared experience, though we remain our separate selves."

Just as with validation, empathizing doesn't necessitate that you share the same feelings or even agree that your partner should feel the way she does. It's not that you're giving up your own feelings or perspective. Rather, you're enhancing your own experience by allowing yourself, for a short period of time, to be emotionally receptive to your partner's experience. What's more, as you've learned, when you feel empathy your body releases more oxytocin and vasopressin into your system, which enhances your sense of comfort and security *and* decreases your anxiety. The degree of empathy present in your relationship greatly affects the degree of connection and goodwill you experience toward your partner *and* your overall sense of well-being. Indeed, empathy is one of the strongest ways to reveal, express, and cement connection. As Hendrix and Hunt (ibid.) assert, "Embracing rather than resisting my partner's experience is the key to deep connection with my love."

Getting to a place of empathy is easier said than done—particularly when you are stressed or in conflict with your partner. Recall, for example, the conflict between Michelle and Tim over the kitchen repairs. Michelle felt that they needed to eat out while their kitchen was being repaired, but Tim felt that this was unnecessary. He became exasperated with Michelle's insistence on what he saw as a frivolous expense and her refusal to be reasoned with. For Michelle, on the other hand, preparing food in the midst of the construction and likely contamination was highly anxiety provoking. She saw eating out as a necessary expense, not a frivolity. That Tim would neither understand nor acquiesce to her need upset Michelle and added to her mounting anxiety and sense of overwhelm. While their differing viewpoints brought about the initial source of dissent, Michelle and Tim's lack of empathy for one another fed the serious gridlock and rupture in connection that followed.

EXERCISE 6.3
Soften Your Heart

This exercise helps you access empathy by softening your heart to your partner. Because it's easier to soften your heart to a child than an adult, you can gain compassion and empathy for your partner by envisioning times when, as a child, your partner needed to be loved, understood, or supported. Now, as a wise, calm adult who is able to provide the nurturing your partner needed back then, you will comfort and support the little child. To make this exercise even more powerful, we suggest that you use childhood memories your partner has shared with you.

Either record this script or ask a friend or therapist to read it to you. Then find a quiet space, and do a closed eye roll (exercise 2.3) and four-square breathing (exercise 2.5) to relax before you begin.

Once you feel relaxed, imagine seeing your partner as a young child—seven or younger. Take a moment to call to mind the image of your partner as this small child.... You probably have seen pictures of your partner as a child and heard stories that can prompt your imagination. Where do you see the child? At home, in the kitchen, in the backyard, at school? What is the child wearing? What do the child's posture and facial expression convey? Once you have captured a sense of this child, hold that image in your mind's eye. Imagine what that child was like—how the child was hurt—what that little child needed—but didn't get from the family.

And once you have called these things to mind, perhaps you can even imagine how you, as an adult, would like to have helped that child—if you had been there when your partner was so young, small, and vulnerable—if you had you been the child's parent. Now take that little child's hand and go together to your safe place, the safe place where you go in your daily stress inoculation, that provides you such comfort—a place that can now be a safe haven for both of you. And once there, ask the little child what he or she would like to do there. Depending on where your safe place is, maybe the child would like to go for a walk, play a game, listen to a story, or walk on the beach. Or perhaps that little child would just like to sit on your lap, relaxing in your arms—finding safety, comfort, and protection as you sit quietly together.

And you can listen to what this young child wants to tell you—and intuitively sense what he needs. Is that little child frightened—or lost, ashamed, and guilty—or hungry for care, affection, or recognition? Or maybe the child got too much: too much attention and not enough space, too much permission and not enough boundaries; too much protection and not enough support of independence and exploration. Whatever it was, this little child wanted to be comforted, seen, heard, accepted, and understood—to feel safe, wanted, and attended to. You can comfort the little child and soften the hurt with your kind, wise, and loving presence. Take another moment or two to stay with these feelings of compassion for the child.

And when you are ready, take a couple of slow, deep breaths and shift your attention to your partner now, as an adult. The very same feelings of compassion and empathy you felt toward the child can open your heart to your partner's adult self—making it easier for you to understand that so many of your partner's defenses, those behaviors that you find so aggravating, come out of that childhood wound. And while those behaviors may still cause you pain, hurt, and frustration—now you can have an added sense of compassion, love, care, patience, and tolerance for them. And when you feel ready to bring this exercise to a close, count slowly from one to twenty, taking all the time you need to open your eyes.

For example, Tim had told Michelle that in his childhood he often had been the caretaker of his mother and siblings. So when Michelle did this exercise, she imagined Tim as a little boy coming home after school to a mother who was sick in bed, a toddler whose diapers needed changing, and two little brothers who needed help with their homework. Michelle felt deep compassion for the little boy who thought he had to fix everything in his family but rarely got the help and guidance he himself needed. When she visualized herself comforting the young Tim, she gained an appreciation for Tim's current tendency to expect everyone to be as pragmatic and stoic as he was—impatiently dismissing anything he considered a frivolity. She also found great satisfaction in offering the little boy she imagined a sense of safety and care. Like Michelle, you may discover that after envisioning your partner as a vulnerable child, you will more easily shift from judgment to compassion for your partner.

Interacting with Empathy

When you empathize, your partner no longer has to carry the weight of his emotions alone. Mediator and professor Gregorio Billikopf Encina (2006) puts it beautifully: "Empathic listening requires that we accompany a person in her moment of sadness, anguish, self-discovery, challenge (or even great joy!)." Your empathy lessens your partner's stress and defensiveness. The following are some strategies to enhance your ability to empathize with your partner.

What to Do When You Just Don't Feel Like Empathizing

Yes, empathizing is beneficial for you and your partner, but how do you empathize with your partner when you feel angry, anxious, stressed, or panicked? Or when you're angry and anxious in reaction to your partner's lack of empathy for *your* experience? You might think, *Why should I empathize with her when she's not doing the same for me?* Even when you are upset or resentful, remember that change can begin with you. Rather than wait for your partner to take the first step, you can create the very feeling you yearn for by empathizing with your partner. Doing so simultaneously defuses tension and changes the dynamics of your interaction by allowing you to model the caring and support that you want.

EXERCISE 6.4
Empathize When It's Hard

You already know how to turn on the empathy switch in your heart by remembering your feelings toward your partner as a young child in need. Sometimes, though, you need an extra kick start. When you find that you just can't bring yourself to elicit empathy, take the following steps:

1. Acknowledge your negative feelings to yourself, along with the situation from which they arose. For example, you might think to yourself, *I can't stand that he keeps interrupting me.*

2. Accept your feelings without judging yourself or your partner. For example, you might say to yourself, *I'm irritated by his interruption. I notice my irritation. I understand it. And I accept my irritation with compassion and without reactivity.*

3. Use your hands-together cue that you established in exercise 6.2 to remind yourself that the negative emotions can coexist right alongside the positive. You can feel impatient *and* tolerant, hurt *and* understanding.

4. Ground yourself with some four-square breathing. Begin to shift your focus to the sense of relaxation and serenity the four-square breaths bring.

5. Finally, when you're feeling calm, allow positive feelings to come to the forefront, helping you prepare to access empathy and compassion for your partner.

Setting an Intention

The intentions we create powerfully affect our thoughts, attitudes, and behaviors. The first step in practicing empathy is to set an intention to be emotionally present for your partner. In doing so, you commit to creating an emotionally safe, welcoming environment in which your partner can be authentic and open with you, a space in which your partner's emotions can be not just heard, but also held. Indeed, the intention to create this environment for your partner is the basis for the expression and reception of empathy. Take the following steps to set this intention to be emotionally present to your partner:

1. Do a closed eye roll, take a few deep breaths to deepen your sense of centeredness, and tell yourself, *I am open to receiving the thoughts and feelings of my partner; I intend to open my heart.* Repeat this intention to yourself as many times as you need.

2. Invoke a sense of compassion and caring for your partner by bringing your right hand to your heart. This is the cue that you created earlier in this chapter to revivify the feelings of warmth and love toward your partner that you identified in exercise 6.1.

Empathic Nonverbal Language

Empathy, like most feelings, is expressed less by what you say than by how you say it. Research suggests that most communication is nonverbal, conveyed by body language: facial expressions, posture, eye movements, and gestures. The tone and pitch of your voice, and the tempo of your speech, compose your *vocal expression*. Mele Koneya and Alton Barbour (1976), authors of *Louder Than Words: Nonverbal Communication*, report that 55 percent of any communication is conveyed through body language and 38 percent through vocal expression. Only 7 percent of communication occurs verbally. So when you convey compassion and empathy to your partner, it's important that your words and nonverbal language are congruent with your intended message.

Communicative Body Movements

The following recommendations for effective nonverbal communication give your partner cues that you are attending to and care about what she is experiencing.

- Establishing and maintaining eye contact conveys your interest in what your partner is expressing, as does leaning slightly toward your partner while you are listening and speaking.

- A soft, welcoming smile conveys caring, as does gently holding your partner's hand or resting your palm on her knee or shoulder.

- Mirroring your partner's posture and gestures, without being mocking, can increase a sense of rapport and synchronicity. It's important to listen actively, using body movements to signal that you are in tune with your partner.

- Gently nodding your head in response to something your partner expresses also shows that you are actively attending to her.

Vocal Communication

The following vocal communication cues effectively convey that you support and welcome your partner's expression. (Please note, however, that exaggerating any of these indicators in a well-intentioned attempt to be extra empathic is likely to come across as forced and inauthentic.)

- Speak quietly, slowly, and in a pitch in the lower register of your natural speaking voice. When you speak in higher tones and with a faster pace, your partner may sense that you are worried or feel rushed. Modulated tones are optimal, as they give your partner more room for emotional expression. Speaking in calm tones creates balance and calm within you as well, sending a message to your own nervous system that everything's okay.

- To establish rapport, let the rhythm, pace, and tone of your responses be similar to those of your partner's speech. However, you certainly wouldn't want to do this if your partner were yelling or speaking in a sarcastic, belittling, or contemptuous manner. If your partner is speaking with too much harshness or intensity, shift the energy of the interaction by softening your own voice. In this way, you can influence the tone and quality of your interaction, keeping the atmosphere of receptivity that you have established.

- Supportive vocal utterances such as "uh-huh," "ah," "mmm," and "oh" are fine if they feel natural to you. Your responsiveness lets your partner know that you're right there emotionally with him. It's one more indicator that you are paying attention and are emotionally invested in his experience. As constructive as sympathetic utterances are, however, only use them when they are authentic in the moment. There's nothing like a feigned "oh" or "mmm" to give your partner the impression that you aren't connecting at all.

Empathic Verbal Language

The key to empathic verbal responses is having the ability to pick up on both verbal and nonverbal communication from your partner. Just as you need to pay attention to what your body movements and vocal tone communicate, you need to be observant of the nonverbal cues your partner is giving you. Remember, it's not just what your partner says; it's how she says it. If you only pay attention to the verbal content of your partner's message and miss out on the emotional expression that underlies it, your own verbal response might be off the mark.

As your partner is speaking to you, notice what feelings you sense she is experiencing. It's perfectly okay to guess at this, as long as you don't make assumptions. When your partner pauses, make your best guess and ask if you're correct. Acknowledging that you care whether or not you are correct is another indicator of your desire to understand your partner.

1. Make statements such as, "I can imagine you are feeling…," "It must be hard for you to…," or "I can sense that you might be feeling…," which indicate that you are listening but are not claiming to know for a fact what your partner is feeling.

2. Next, follow your comment with a check-in, such as, "Does that resonate with you?" or "Does that feel right to you?" This gives your partner a chance to clarify, as well as elaborate.

By venturing a guess followed by checking in, you demonstrate that you're attempting to pick up on your partner's emotional experience without imposing your own interpretations. Remember, empathizing is about being *with* your partner as she expresses whatever thoughts and emotions she is experiencing—not analyzing, not solving problems, not fixing. It can be tempting to step in and offer solutions or assurance by presenting a different perspective.

When you do this, however, you're no longer being *with* your partner's emotional experience. It's likely that there have been many times when your partner has stepped in with solutions, when you've actually just wanted to feel heard and supported. By sticking to brief guesses and check-ins, you're giving your partner the opportunity to have that very experience.

Wrapping It Up

When you and your partner are in conflict, feelings of love, caring, and warmth may seem to simply turn off. Having learned to generate and express compassion and empathy toward your partner, you can keep these feelings flowing even during conflict. In doing so, that sense of alienation and isolation will leave, even when you disagree with your partner. The rewarding aspects of your relationship—the sense of partnership, care, and connection—needn't vanish just because you are in dispute. Feelings of compassion soften your anger, hurt, and mounting anxiety and allow you to connect to your partner's endearing qualities. And by generating and expressing empathy, you join your partner in overcoming feelings of disconnect and opposition. It is from this place that productive, loving dialogue can both resolve conflict and increase intimacy.

part 3

TAKING IT
TO THE
NEXT LEVEL

chapter 7

Moving toward Healthy Interdependence

As Anita walked back to her house from the mailbox, one envelope in particular caught her eye. It was addressed to her husband and carried the return address of a medical lab. Immediately, Anita felt the familiar sense of fear and anxiety begin to surge. The worries that used to be her constant companion cascaded: *Mike didn't tell me he'd had lab work. What is he hiding from me? What if he's really sick? What if he has cancer?*

Recognizing that her anxiety was triggered, Anita reasoned with herself as she headed straight to her home office for a brief time-out: *I don't have to get all bent out of shape over this. A lot of my fear just comes from my maximizing. I don't have any real evidence to believe that Mike's seriously ill right now. I just know that he had some tests—that's it. What I really need to do right now is calm down. After my time-out, I'll figure out how to approach this with Mike. But I can't do anything until I get myself calm first.*

By the time Anita finished her time-out, her anxiety level had eased. Able to engage her rational forebrain, she remembered that she needed to wait to have the difficult conversation until she and

Mike both felt calm and emotionally available. Since dinnertime would be the first chance for Mike to relax and wind down after work, Anita decided to wait until after dinner to ask about the medical testing.

As dinner came to a close, Anita again invoked her new communication skills. Instead of immediately launching into her worries, she asked Mike if he was open to hearing something that was on her mind. He agreed.

"You got a bill in the mail today from a medical lab. It's from the same company where I had blood work done last year. What's going on?"

"It was nothing." Mike's reply was calm and matter of fact. Seeing that Anita was expecting more, he continued guardedly. "It really wasn't anything you need to worry about. I had some pain in my back, so I went to the doctor and he ran some lab work. It turns out I had a slight kidney infection, and he put me on antibiotics— end of story. I finished the antibiotics a week ago, and now I'm as good as new. It's all over and done with. I thought I gave them my office for the billing address; I'm sorry you saw that bill. It's really nothing you need to concern yourself about." Like many people with a partner who struggles with high anxiety, Mike had avoided confiding in Anita because he knew it would trigger her anxiety.

"I understand where you're coming from," Anita replied with warmth in her voice. "And if it were a year ago, you would have been absolutely right; my worries would've gone straight through the roof. I'd have panicked that I was going to lose you. Before, I would've called you at work demanding an explanation, and you would've had to stop everything to talk me down off the ledge."

"You know, you just about outlined exactly why I didn't tell you anything." Mike seemed to relax a bit. "I love you, honey, and I know you really well. I wasn't going to do that to you. There was no reason to worry you."

Anita took a moment to take in Mike's comment. Incorporating what she'd learned about communication, she wanted to express her empathy for Mike's predicament. "I hear that you didn't want to worry me, and I appreciate your consideration. It's true, my first response today when I got that bill was to panic, but I have tools now to calm myself down. The point I want to make," Anita continued, "is that I want you to be able to tell me those things now. It's not your job to talk me off the ledge or to hide things from me that you think will throw me off balance. I know that in the past, I've looked to you to do that, and you're really good at being the rock when I'm on edge. But I don't want that anymore; it's not good for me, and it's not good for you."

No longer powerless in the face of her anxiety, Anita was ready for her relationship to grow and shift. She had identified a common dynamic that exists when one partner has high anxiety and the other doesn't: one partner becomes the "rock," seeking to protect the other from her anxiety. The bonds that form in this kind of dynamic can be very strong. Given some of the views on romantic relationships that exist in our culture, this type of bond may even seem ideal. However, many of these overdependent relationships, although apparently stable, are far from ideal.

Debunking the Romantic Myth

You've probably heard the international best-selling hit song "Without You," which has been covered by numerous recording artists since it was written in 1970 by Pete Ham and Tom Evans of the rock group Badfinger. Mariah Carey revived the song in the mid-1990s by belting out those famous lyrics about feeling hopelessly unable to live without a particular person in your life. The song spells out a popular conception of romantic love: romantic union as a fusion of sorts, with two halves coming together to make a whole. In the movie Jerry Maguire (Crowe 1996), Renée Zellweger's character, Dorothy, famously proves her love for Tom Cruise's Jerry Maguire by declaring, "You complete me." In this popular view of romance, each lover is incomplete, insufficient without the other. The romantic partnership allows two incomplete selves to unite, fusing together in a partnership that provides them the ability to function in the world that each would otherwise lack.

The message that can be taken from "Without You," Shakespeare's *Romeo and Juliet*, and most romantic movies is that cessation of the romantic relationship equals cessation of the self. "I don't know who I'd be without you," "I don't know what I'd do without you," "I don't know how I'd live without you," and the even more dramatic, "I can't live without you," are common ways lovers tell one another the depth of their love, commitment, and passion. But this type of love, this powerful, all-encompassing, mutually dependent emotional fusion, prized as the pinnacle of true love, isn't all it's made out to be. The *Romeo and Juliet* ideal is, in fact, no ideal at all.

The Continuum of Dependency

In romantic relationships the degree of the partners' dependency falls on a continuum, with *overdependence* at one end and *extreme independence* at the other. The middle ground between these two extremes is healthy *interdependence*, the dynamic we encourage couples to aim for. By staying within this middle ground, your partnership will greatly enhance your sense of well-being, satisfaction, and security without diminishing your sense of self.

Being able to depend on yourself enhances your sense of connection, togetherness, and well-being, and it prevents the relationship from swinging to the overdependent end of the spectrum. Equally important, being able to depend on your partner at times for a sense of well-being, security, and reassurance prevents the relationship from swinging to the other end of the continuum, extreme independence. Healthy interdependence shows up in the difference between the sentiments, "I don't know how I'd live without you" (overdependence) and, "I don't need you for anything" (extreme independence). Healthy interdependence exists in the sentiment, "I have the innate ability to live a rewarding and fulfilling life, *and* my life is wonderfully enhanced by my partnership with you," as indicated in the following diagram.

Continuum of Dependency

Overdependence   Healthy   Extreme
                   Interdependence   Independence

Anxiety and the Continuum of Dependency

When heightened anxiety enters a relationship, the dynamics between partners often shift toward the overdependent end of the spectrum. Before learning the time-out and daily-stress-inoculation tools that give you control of your anxiety levels, it's natural to look to your partner for the strength, reassurance, and stability that chronic anxiety steals from you. However, when you rely on your partner's emotional support rather than on your own internal resources to regulate your anxiety, you're making your partner, not you, responsible for your emotional well-being. When this dynamic arises, the relationship bond becomes overdependent.

Now that's not to say that you shouldn't look to your partner as a source of emotional support. Indeed, one hallmark of a healthy, interdependent relationship is the ability of each partner to go to the other for comfort. By using the tools in this book, you can achieve another hallmark of an interdependent relationship: an ability to manage your own levels of anxiety, resulting in a greater sense of personal strength and resiliency. Of course, your relationship with your partner should also be a source of reassurance and comfort. A successful relationship artfully balances individuality and mutuality. This is the crux of that healthy middle ground of interdependence.

In this optimal scenario you're not running to your partner when your anxiety levels are on red alert, expecting him to talk you down. Indeed, the expectation that your partner could and should talk you down gets relationships in hot water. Even if you're fortunate enough to have selected a partner who will consistently calm your anxiety, this comes at a great cost to both of you. You're depriving yourself of the opportunity to develop your own self-soothing and self-validation skills and to know your own strengths and abilities.

Heightened anxiety can also foster dependency in the way that you and your partner share tasks and responsibilities. You may avoid tasks, situations, or activities such as grocery shopping or even holding a full-time job, because they might trigger your anxiety. Your partner may be willing to protect you from anxiety by picking up the slack—agreeing to do all the grocery shopping or to be the primary breadwinner in order to compensate for your anxiety. It may seem harmless, yet by relying on your partner rather than developing the skills to overcome your anxiety, you're allowing your anxiety to dictate both your life *and* that of your partner. Overdependence results.

The key to sharing household responsibilities is to capitalize on each partner's strengths. Maybe you love cooking and your partner has neither the knack nor the desire to make much beyond canned soup and cold sandwiches. You both might decide that most of the time you will be in charge of cooking and your partner will be in charge of the cleanup. In this case, your strengths, rather than your anxiety, suggest a simple division of labor. You and your partner exemplify interdependence by inquiring, "How are we going to pool our mutual resources to best meet our individual and mutual needs?" This is very different from parceling out responsibilities to compensate for your anxiety.

The Payoff of Overdependent Bonds

Given the many benefits of interdependent bonds, why do so many couples—and specifically couples in which one partner suffers from heightened anxiety—drift into overdependency? An overdependent bond has many payoffs. For one thing, the focus of the relationship—relieving one partner's anxiety—is narrow and rigid, which, paradoxically, makes the relationship stable and predictable. The lack of flexibility gives the relationship consistency. In addition, depending heavily on one another can be deeply gratifying. (Remember the *Romeo and Juliet* myth of relationships.) Perhaps your partner is giving you the care and nurturing that you never got as a child. Or perhaps this caretaking relationship recapitulates the overprotection you received from an anxious parent. Dependence on your partner can feel very good indeed.

Getting into Action: Exercises That Promote Interdependence

Even though it feels safe and comfortable, avoiding that which you fear keeps you stuck in your fear. It also keeps you and your partner stuck in rigid roles regarding who offers support to whom at any given moment, because your anxiety often takes center stage. The next three exercises will help you actively shift into an interdependent bond with your partner.

EXERCISE 7.1
Trust That You're Okay

The first step in this process of shifting the dynamics of your relationship involves strengthening your sense of safety and security in the present moment. Fearing danger at every turn—maximizing and future focusing—can fuel your anxiety and keep you stuck in overdependent patterns of interaction. Learning to trust that everything really is okay in any given moment gives you the resilience, inner strength, and sense of solidity that facilitates healthy interdependence. To help access this sense of resilience, we will revisit and strengthen the "okay" symbol that you created in exercise 5.2. To prepare for this exercise, either record the following script or have a friend or therapist agree to read it to you. Then set aside ten to fifteen minutes in a quiet, comfortable space where you won't be disturbed. When you're ready to begin, do the closed eye roll (exercise 2.3) and four-square breathing (exercise 2.5), and proceed with the following visualization:

> With each exhalation, allow your mind to drift deeper and deeper into a quiet inner state…where your thoughts slow down—as if you were not thinking much at all. And the more you continue to relax, the more you can enjoy that quiet stillness of your inner world. And in this stillness, you can know that you are safe and sound. At this moment— right here, right now—everything is okay.
>
> Perhaps you can notice that you're already feeling calmer and more peaceful than you felt just a few moments ago. Now take a moment to allow a feeling of calm to flow through you and all around you. The only thing you need to think about is the growing comfort of this relaxed state. This is a good time to memorize this feeling of being okay—maybe even more than okay. And

now, once again, you can make your "okay" symbol, which will automatically elicit this state of being whenever you need to. You can use this cue right now by pressing your thumb and forefinger together to form your "okay" symbol. And as you feel your fingers touching, remember that you really are okay.

Continue to hold your thumb and forefinger in the position of the "okay" symbol, and as you do, think the words, I am okay, three times. Even if a part of you doubts that this is completely true, it's important to think these words anyway. When you think the words and make the "okay" symbol, you will cue the sense of well-being you are experiencing right now. And each time in the future that you bring your thumb and forefinger together, you will know that you are okay.

And because you're feeling okay, it is easier for you to acknowledge your own strength and to trust that you have the resources to manage your own fear. It becomes second nature to trust your own inner wisdom. You gain the sense that you are capable and competent—able to respond to the demands of life—inviting your partner to come to you for support at times—and accepting your partner's support without feeling dependent on it. Knowing that you are okay makes it possible to transform your relationship with your partner. Now release your fingers, letting go of the "okay" symbol but retaining the good feelings that emerged. And when you're ready to end this exercise, knowing that you can always call back this feeling of being okay, you can count slowly from one to twenty, taking all the time you need to open your eyes.

Take a minute to come back and slowly open your eyes.

EXERCISE 7.2
Foster Role Flexibility

As mentioned previously, couples in interdependent relationships demonstrate role flexibility that is not found in relationships at either extreme of the dependency continuum. Rather than one partner consistently being the rock, roles shift in response to situations and stressors. You are able to enjoy the freedom to fulfill multiple roles with one another.

Besides maintaining role flexibility, partners in interdependent relationships also recognize that it's important to have meaningful relationships outside the partnership. Relationships with friends and family provide a vital source of support and fulfillment to both of you. No relationship can thrive as an island. It's essential that your partnership isn't your only means of support. This is another component of role flexibility.

In this exercise, you will envision yourself occupying a variety of roles across a number of relationships. To begin, you will need paper and a pen, or, if you prefer, a computer. It's important to actually write or type your responses to the prompts, because this physical act helps you process your thoughts differently than if you simply think them. Additionally, you will use your writing from this exercise to complete exercise 7.3, so make sure to save your journal for later use.

Once you are ready, turn off the phone ringer and find a comfortable place where you won't be disturbed. Center yourself by doing some four-square breathing (see exercise 2.5). When you are relaxed, copy the following prompts and respond to them with specific details.

Ways I can give myself...

Comfort (for example, *Taking yoga classes*): _____

Relaxation: _____

Validation: _____

Joy: _____

Ways friends and family can give me...

Comfort: _____

Relaxation: _____

Validation (for example, *Call a trusted friend when I'm worried*):

_____

Support: _____

Joy: _____

Companionship: _____

Ways I can give my partner...

Comfort (for example, *Giving a massage*): _____

Relaxation: _____

Validation: _____

Joy: _____

Companionship: _____

Compassion: _____

Appreciation: _____

Ways I would like my partner to enhance (not create) my sense of...

Comfort: _____

Relaxation: _____

Validation (for example, *She communicates that she under-stands why I'm worried—even if she's not worried*):

_____

Joy: _____

Companionship: _____

Compassion: _____

Appreciation: _____

EXERCISE 7.3
Enjoy the New Flexibility

Thinking about broadening the range of roles you fill and feeling comfortable doing so are two different things. The mere thought of taking action to inhabit these new roles in your relationships might bring about a great deal of discomfort. Change can be uncomfortable, especially when you're letting go of the notion that your partner has to be your rock all of the time. This exercise can help you experience the gratification that comes from participating in a variety of roles in your relationship. This process is so simple it's laughable—literally.

Putting a smile on your face may be the simplest way to send your brain the message, "All's clear; everything's fine." Scientists have found that we can actually communicate feel-good messages to the brain through the act of smiling. To put it simply, smiling feels good. Researcher Robert Soussignan (2002) has found that smiling is associated with feel-good patterns of autonomic nervous system arousal. As you'll recall from chapter 2, anxiety-related autonomic nervous system arousal is responsible for many of the unpleasant physical sensations associated with heightened anxiety. Smiling literally puts your body and mind at ease. In addition, researcher and psychologist Robert Zajonc and his colleagues (Zajonc 1985; Zajonc, Murphy, and Inglehart 1989) reported that the tightening and relaxing of facial muscles that occurs with smiling can cool the temperature of the blood flowing to the brain, which can make it easier to regulate emotions. The benefits of smiling occur whether the smile is spontaneous or volitional. In both cases, the smile sends a message to your brain that you are comfortable and happy. So even if the smile is forced at first, once you invest in the experience, the smile takes on a life of its own. The comfort and pleasure become yours. And of course, when you are comfortable and happy, it's easier to take risks, to be flexible, and to be less dependent.

157

This exercise uses visualization to reinforce your responses to the entries in the previous exercise with the addition of smiling. Take your time with each step; it typically takes several sittings to complete this exercise. For each scenario (such as *Ways I can give myself comfort*), do the following:

1. Read your written response.

2. Turn your answer into scenes in which you see yourself doing or receiving the actions you wrote down. Visualize in detail whom you're with and where you are. Use all your senses to vivify this experience: note what you hear, what you smell, what you feel in your body.

3. When you feel immersed in this movie clip of your experience, take a deep breath and allow yourself a long, relaxing exhalation. At the end of exhalation, allow a smile to form.

4. Continue to smile as you view your movie clip, even if the smile feels forced at first. Remind yourself of how the simple action of a smile is affecting your emotional state and engendering positive emotions. Even if you don't immediately notice a shift in your mood, you can trust that your smile is sending your brain positive messages that can help you truly enjoy and embrace your role in the scenario you are envisioning.

5. After you've held this image (along with your smile) for a moment or two, let the scene fade away. And as it fades, you can maintain the sense of satisfaction and freedom that comes from this positive experience.

After you've done all the scenes, you can repeat any that you found most helpful.

Wrapping It Up

There's an art to developing and maintaining healthy interdependence in a relationship. Remember the envelope from the medical lab that at one time would have sent Anita into a tailspin of anxiety. In crisis mode, she'd have had to rely on Mike to calm her down. As Anita became able to better tolerate her anxiety and even regulate it, her relationship with Mike matured. As she became less dependent on Mike, their emotional connection deepened. Mike no longer felt that he needed to protect Anita from her own anxiety. Rather than simply be a source of strength for her, Mike discovered that he could even turn to Anita when he was feeling vulnerable. All areas of their relationship grew stronger as a result of Anita's growing ability to manage her anxiety.

Like Anita and Mike, you and your partner will grow closer and more interdependent as you continue to master your anxiety and let go of the illusion that two incomplete selves make a whole. Furthermore, as you both become more flexible and trusting in your roles and expectations of one another, you'll foster healthy interdependence in your relationship.

chapter 8

The Wise Relationship

Healthy interdependence is a major component of the pinnacle of a fulfilling, rewarding romantic relationship: the wise relationship. In this chapter we explain how to weave healthy interdependence into the broader tapestry of the wise relationship. The wise relationship itself is impossible to define in one simple sentence. Rather, it is a constellation of many components that foster a climate of emotional intimacy. In short, it takes healthy interdependence to the next level. This chapter touches on key components of the wise relationship, instilling the knowledge and skills that will bring the wise relationship to fruition. Namely, change your attitude, change your actions, change your relationship.

Attitudes and Thoughts That Support the Wise Relationship

Stepping into the wise relationship involves a paradigm shift in the way you approach your partner and conceptualize your relationship. In essence, you're redefining the rules of engagement by shifting your attitudes and changing your thoughts so that they support what you value: a healthy, solid relationship. The more you think about and express the following attitudes, the more easily your actions will shift to help you create a wise relationship. This section articulates three perspectives that support this shift: finding satisfaction in "not perfect but good enough," letting go of the need to be right, and letting go of the illusion of fairness.

Finding Satisfaction in "Not Perfect but Good Enough"

"Someday my prince will come" is a fantasy that just about every little girl has had at one time or another. The reality is that few princes (or princesses) actually exist. Even if you find yourself with the person of your dreams, there will be bumps in the road. The tough reality is that when you are in a long-term relationship, you inevitably experience disillusionment. You find out that your prince or princess has flaws that you were unaware of or ignored during your courtship. If you were expecting perfection, you'll surely be disappointed. If the gap between your expectations and reality is wide, you may even spiral into despair. The truth is that every partner and every relationship has flaws. Satisfaction in your intimate relationship is directly connected to your ability to accept, even embrace, these imperfections. In a rewarding and successful relationship—a wise relationship—the connection between you and your partner is not perfect, but *good enough.*

As you'll recall from chapter 4, the experience of attuned connection, that deeply fulfilling experience of emotional resonance with your partner, is essential in an intimate relationship. However, attuned connection is not a constant. In even the best relationships, there are ruptures during which this connection breaks and the partners are out of sync with one another. After observing the ebb and flow of attuned connection in mother-child relationships, British psychoanalyst Donald Winnicott (1953) coined the term "the good-enough mother." He saw that healthy, emotionally nourishing bonds occurred when the mother and child experienced attunement and repair when there was a rupture in connection. Perfection on the part of the mother isn't possible or, it turns out, even needed. The successful mother is the one who is "good enough": able to make mistakes, weather the distress that ruptures bring, and then reestablish connection with her child.

We can apply Winnicott's findings of the good-enough mother to your intimate partnership. Rather than the perfect relationship, find satisfaction in your "good-enough" relationship with your "good-enough" partner. By accepting that you and your partner naturally fall in and out of attunement, you can create an environment in which you both feel that it's safe to let go of the expectation of perfection. You know that you will have missteps. You will butt heads. You will feel misheard and misunderstood. You will feel frustrated by one another. This is part of any enduring intimate relationship, as are the resulting uncomfortable emotions. When ruptures occur, your relationship is not over; your attunement is just momentarily broken.

In the wise relationship you acknowledge and accept the discomfort of these experiences of rupture, knowing that you have the tools (such as time-outs and self-validation) to tolerate the difficult emotions and that you have the communication skills to repair the connection. With this understanding, you both give and receive the gift that the other doesn't have to be perfect to be loved. It becomes okay to be good enough.

To help you establish this attitude, repeat to yourself the statement, *When I accept that my partner will never be perfect, I can appreciate that my partner and my relationship are good enough.*

Letting Go of the Need to Be Right

Another attitude key to enjoying a wise relationship is accepting the remarkable truth that you don't always have to be right. In fact, insistence on being right is counter to the cooperative spirit of a wise relationship. Indeed, it often elicits equal rigidity from your partner. Peter T. McIntyre, an author and artist in the 1700s, wisely said, "Confidence comes not from always being right but from not fearing being wrong." The willingness to be wrong makes a wise relationship possible.

Therapists often ask their client couples who are in conflict, "Would you rather be right, or would you rather be in a relationship?" Although you would probably answer that you want a relationship, your actions may at times reflect a greater desire to be right. For instance, in conversation with your partner, do you dig in your heels and insist that your opinion is right? Letting go of the need to be right, even if only by agreeing to disagree, is an essential skill in the wise relationship.

To reinforce this new attitude, repeat to yourself the statement, *Because I value my relationship, I let go of the need to always be right.*

Letting Go of the Illusion of Fairness

In chapter 7 we discussed the importance of sharing and delegating responsibilities. This is an essential component of a wise relationship. However, if you get too caught up in the idea of *fairness*—that each of you has to assume a perfectly equal share—you will end up stewing with resentment. There is seldom perfect fairness, and focusing on it is a guarantee of disappointment. The key to sharing responsibilities is to allow flexibility, generosity, and a sense of partnership to trump resentment over perceived inequalities.

To strengthen this attitude, repeat to yourself the statement, *Because I want a wise relationship, I find it easy to let go of my need for everything to be fair.*

Actions That Support the Wise Relationship

A popular riddle poses this question: Three frogs were sitting on a log. One decided to jump off. How many frogs were left on the log? If you answered, "Two frogs," think again. The one frog only *decided* to jump off the log. Deciding to do something and actually taking action are two different things. By adopting the thoughts and attitudes expressed in the previous section, you're preparing yourself to take action and make the jump into the wise relationship. Indeed, the right attitudes are essential, as they give you the foundation necessary to support the actions you will take. The actions outlined in this section, however, provide the final step—or leap—toward achieving the wise relationship you desire.

Refraining from Hurtful Communication

An important component of the wise relationship is a mutual awareness of the double-edged power of words to harm or soothe. Once, an older woman was asked to divulge the secret to the success of her sixty-year marriage. She responded, "At least three times a day, I *don't* say something." What you don't say has as much impact on your intimate relationship as what you do say.

Knowing how much and how little to disclose to your partner is a mark of a wise relationship. In chapters 4 and 5 you learned skills to help you respond rather than react to your partner, to engage in constructive dialogue, to validate and empathize with your partner, and to allow for differences of opinion. Next you need to learn how to determine when to refrain from disclosure to your partner.

When motives such as blaming or shaming color your communication, speaking your thoughts can cause hurt, incite conflict, or shut down your partner's emotional receptiveness. Harsh, negative communication, though indeed a form of disclosure, is not an aspect of the wise relationship. In fact, research shows that it can do permanent damage to your relationship. Researcher and relationship expert John Gottman (2000) has identified four patterns of behavior in partnerships that predict the ultimate breakup of the relationship. He calls these predictors the "Four Horsemen of the Apocalypse." One of them is partners' criticism and condemnation of one another.

With that caution in mind, before you let your tongue fly, check your motives. If your motives include any of the following *and* you want your relationship to last, the better part of wisdom is to bite your tongue:

- Criticizing

- Blaming

- Shaming

- Devaluing

- Expressing contempt

- Avoiding your own shame

Refraining from making that biting remark is *not* underdisclosing or withholding pertinent information. By holding your tongue in the heat of the moment and later engaging your partner using the communication techniques you've learned, you will be able to strengthen the trust and connection that underlie a wise relationship.

With your anxiety in check, you will discover satisfaction in holding your tongue. You will not only notice a positive impact on your relationship, but also experience the satisfaction of self-restraint and self-control.

To reinforce your intention to hold your tongue, repeat to yourself this statement: *After I take a few relaxing breaths, it's easier to release the impulse to use judgmental words.*

Accessing Your Inner Wisdom

An ability to access and act on your inner wisdom is a component of the wise relationship related to experiencing attunement and engaging in role flexibility. In exercises 7.2 and 7.3 you gained a sense of the multiple roles you and your partner can fulfill in your relationship. Yet how do you sense when to inhabit what role? How do you know when to be the one to give support and when to be the one to ask for comforting? The answer comes with developing your ability to access your own inner wisdom. In doing so, it's essential to learn to distinguish the voice of inner wisdom from the urges and desires that are driven by fear-based needs.

Fear is a powerful motivator that influences your actions and perceived needs. When you're at the mercy of your anxiety, fear can drown out that wise inner voice. As you continue your daily stress inoculation and time-outs, however, you will find that fear will lose its grip over you, and you will gain greater access to an inner voice that transcends fear-based self-guidance. When you're not blindsided by fear, you are better able to hear that intuitive inner voice that picks up on your partner's moods and helps you sense and respond to your partner's needs. In the wise relationship, both partners draw from this intuitive inner wisdom to meet each other's needs; role flexibility occurs with an ease made possible by this access to inner wisdom and a willingness to act on this inner guidance.

To reinforce your intention to access and act on your inner wisdom, repeat to yourself this statement: *I call forth my inner wisdom to guide and support me.*

Sealing the Deal with Gratitude

In the wise relationship, there is mutual appreciation and gratitude. Most relationship experts, including John Gottman, Harville Hendrix, and Patricia Love, emphasize the importance of mutual appreciation between partners, identifying it as an essential ingredient in good relationships. When you focus on appreciation, feelings of gratitude automatically emerge. And gratitude, an internal state, leads to a feeling of well-being. We know that people who are grateful are happier (Emmons and McCullough 2003). We have also observed that when you focus on what you are grateful for in your partner, your relationship improves. Your partner will sense your gratitude and is likely to reciprocate. Melody Beattie (1990, 32), well-known self-help expert on codependence, writes, "Gratitude is the key that turns problems into blessings and the unexpected into gifts." The following exercise helps you access feelings of gratitude.

EXERCISE 8.1
Nurture Gratitude

At least three times a day, do this exercise. The following script will guide you through the process:

Take a moment to stop and think about something you appreciate about your partner. As you think about it, let yourself smile—and let gratitude arise. And as you begin to experience this gratitude and appreciation, notice how satisfying this feels. Let yourself really enjoy the satisfaction—becoming more and more aware of how good it feels to be grateful.

Hold on to this sense of satisfaction for a minute or two—really allowing yourself to enjoy this self-directed shift in your emotional state. The choice is yours to let yourself feel the satisfaction of that appreciation. Really feel it—knowing that as you do, you nurture yourself and your relationship.

And now, make a commitment that three times a day, you will appreciate something about your partner: when you get up in the morning, as you daydream for a moment in the middle of the day, and just before you go to sleep at night.

You may not always feel like doing this—but as you continue to commit to this practice, you'll find that appreciation and gratitude become more and more accessible. And perhaps in the future, your default mode will be gratitude. And as you continue to switch the gratitude button on in your mind and hold on to these feelings, you can look forward to the pleasure of good feelings. You may even be surprised at how easy it becomes to be more aware of your gratitude—and look forward to reducing conflict and deepening your connection with your partner.

Wrapping It Up

A wise relationship is ever changing. In many ways, the course of a wise relationship can be compared to the cycles in the life of a garden. To flourish, gardens need a watchful eye. The gardener has to weed and fertilize. Shifts in the weather and seasons without blossoms all call for patience and trust. The gardener must carefully protect the garden against outside harm. With each season, the gardener knows to thoroughly enjoy and be grateful for the fruits of his labor. The next chapter will give you the tools and strategies to maintain the fruits of your efforts, to manage your anxiety, and to grow the garden of your wise relationship.

chapter 9

Maintaining the Fruits of Your Labor

"Practice makes perfect," the popular adage goes. In regard to the skills you've learned in this book, however, it's more accurate to say, "Practice makes permanent." By continuing to apply the skills you've learned, you will be rewarded with lasting change. By taking the following final steps to solidify your new skills, you will ensure that you will benefit from the fruits of your labor for endless seasons to come.

Practice Makes Permanent

Regulating your anxiety every day with time-outs and the daily stress inoculation you learned in part 1 is essential to managing your anxiety. To maintain your connection to your partner and transform that relationship, you also need to be consistent in practicing the strategies taught in parts 2 and 3. This is like learning a new language. When you want to learn a new language, you need to speak it every day to become fluent. Without regular practice, speaking with ease is almost impossible.

This truism about changing our behavior is backed by science. Neuroscientists have found that practicing a new skill strengthens the neuronal pathways in the brain associated with the skill (Goleman 2011; Siegel 2012). This is like strengthening a muscle: the more repetitions, the stronger the muscle becomes. And, just as a muscle becomes weak again when you stop exercising, the neuronal connections that support the skill weaken when you stop practicing it. With this in mind, the following exercise builds on the anxiety-regulating skills you learned in chapter 3 and the role-flexibility exercises you carried out in chapter 7. It will help you maintain the skills you've learned so that you can enjoy the rewards of your hard work: a life with less anxiety and an enhanced connection with your partner.

EXERCISE 9.1
Expand Your Nightly Visualization

Exercise 3.4 taught you how to harness the power of intention to help you engage in your daily stress inoculation. With only a minute or two of visualization, you learned to set an intention and enhance the likelihood that your future actions will support that intention. As we discussed, when it comes to the power of intention, seeing really *is* believing, and believing leads to doing. And finally, repeatedly doing an action creates a new habit.

This exercise has a twofold purpose: to set an intention to enhance your relationship and to experience the rewarding emotions that result from visualizing positive interactions with your partner. The emotions that arise during the visualization are a powerful motivator in themselves, reinforcing your intention and new behaviors. You can do this exercise after completing the nightly visualization in exercise 3.4 by adding the following steps:

1. When you are already in a relaxed state, lying comfortably in your bed, choose a relationship-enhancing behavior that you want to master. For example, you might select providing your partner support, expressing appreciation, or validating your partner's perspective even if you don't agree with it. You might also use a scenario you wrote about in your journal in exercise 7.2.

2. As if you were watching a video clip of this ideal interaction between you and your partner, visualize yourself engaging in the relationship-enhancing behavior you selected.

   See the scene in detail: Hear yourself speaking calmly and respectfully—with words that come from your wise self. Maybe you see yourself looking at your partner with loving compassion or simple appreciation. Can you see yourself nodding your head in understanding? Smiling? Maybe you are laughing appreciatively. Have fun with this as you create the scene that showcases your ideal behavior.

   As you continue to visualize the scenario, enjoy the positive, rewarding feelings of connection and compassion that come from this imagined interaction with your partner. You can even savor the satisfaction of knowing that you are capable of transforming your relationship by engaging in new behaviors. And after enjoying the positive emotions and knowing you can continue to hold on to them, you can open your eyes.

Highlights and Tips for Moving Forward

The following tips will help you sustain the progress you have made in reducing your anxiety and transforming your relationship with your partner. They are a summary of your learning throughout the three parts of this book. Keep this list handy, and perhaps even make copies that you can post in your house and office as reminders. (There is also an abridged list in appendix C).

Dialing Down Your Distress (Part 1)

Know your triggers. It's important to remain alert to the internal and external triggers that indicate your anxiety may be on the rise. Some stressors will remain consistent, others will change over time, and new ones may emerge.

Don't miss the bus. The optimal time for a time-out is right when you notice a trigger, not five minutes later, when your anxiety has escalated. By stopping your anxiety in its tracks, you don't give it a chance to intensify.

See it as a gift. You are more likely to continue to practice the daily stress inoculation if you view it as a gift to yourself rather than a chore. Perspective is everything.

Just do your best. Success doesn't require perfection—it's just about doing your best. You won't always enact your time-outs perfectly. You might not maintain perfect consistency with your daily stress inoculation. Don't beat yourself up about it, and don't let it derail you. Tomorrow's another day.

Connecting with the One You Love (Part 2)

Chill first. Take a time-out to get calm and restore optimal communication between your emotion-based midbrain and logic-based forebrain before discussing conflict with your partner. You want to communicate, not vent.

When cabin pressure's low, don't rely on your partner to put your oxygen mask on you. Remember, you can give yourself compassion, soothing, and validation. Listen to your inner voice and acknowledge that your needs are valid. Sometimes your partner won't be available or will fail to meet your needs. Remember that role flexibility, including meeting your own needs, is part of a healthy interdependent relationship.

Timing is everything. Before initiating a difficult conversation, make sure both you and your partner are in a good mind-set. Remember, your partner hasn't necessarily taken a time-out. Check in with your partner before you launch into conversation to see if he feels calm enough to communicate constructively.

Take a lesson from kids and cats. Children and cats are naturally curious. When you feel emotionally reactive and judgmental toward your partner, challenge yourself to be curious about your partner's perspective instead. Put yourself in your partner's shoes and be open to a different perspective. A stance of curiosity opens new possibilities and creates a feeling of safety and acceptance for you and your partner.

A spoonful of sugar helps. Start your dialogue by describing what you appreciate about your partner. It's tempting to launch straight into the negative when you're in the middle of a dispute. It will be easier for your partner to receive your feedback when you say it in a context of appreciation and positive regard. And, starting with something positive reminds you of why you chose to be in a relationship with this person in the first place—and why you still want to be.

Don't play tennis during conversations with your partner. Discussing conflicts is not like playing tennis, where each of you bats the ball back and forth. Make an agreement with your partner to allow each other to complete everything each of you wants to say before the other responds. Resist the urge to interrupt and interject your side of the story, and don't spend your listening time formulating your rebuttal.

Taking It to the Next Level (Part 3)

Try on a number of hats. In interdependent relationships, role flexibility is important. While it might feel like you're going against the grain, flexibility in roles indicates a healthy relationship, just as a flexible spine indicates a healthy body.

Prince or Princess Charming doesn't live here. In real life, "happily ever after" includes inevitable ruptures and repairs in attuned connection. The ultimate satisfaction in relationships occurs when you accept this reality and embrace the wise, good-enough relationship.

How do you get to Carnegie Hall? Practice, practice, practice. Every day, exercise the self-regulation and communication muscles you've developed. This is the only way to maintain the skills you've learned that have resulted in the enhanced connection with your partner that you now enjoy. And remember, each hurdle you face in the future can add to your growth, as long as you continue to practice the exercises in this book.

Keep this book handy! You will inevitably face challenges in managing your anxiety and staying in healthy connection with your partner. We strongly encourage you to refer back to this book in those situations. Rather than kick yourself for needing a refresher, take advantage of the help available in these pages.

Wrapping It Up

Anxious in Love is ultimately a journey about progress, not perfection. While you might tend to focus on what you have yet to master, we encourage you to acknowledge and celebrate the victories you have achieved, both small and large, in managing your anxiety and improving your relationship. No longer at the whim of your anxiety, you now have the ability to recognize your triggers and regulate your anxiety levels with time-outs and the daily stress inoculation. You've also gained skills to enhance your communication with, connection to, and compassion for your partner. While this is an ongoing process that will become more refined over time, you can feel good about the strides that you have already made and the effort that you continue to put forth.

Take a moment to notice how your baseline stress level has decreased and that your "red alerts" occur less frequently. Think of an occasion when a time-out has helped you move from reacting to responding. Acknowledge a time when you have validated your partner even when you didn't agree with her point of view, as well as times when you have validated your own perspective. Remember moments when you have felt an abundance of compassion, both for yourself and your partner. In each of those moments, you took a step toward the wise relationship.

Of course, there will always be new challenges and new demands on you and your relationship. However, by continuing to use the tools in this book, you will become increasingly resilient, able to reduce conflict and spring back from whatever life throws at you and your partner. The cumulative effect of these changes in you and your ways of interacting can shift the very dynamic of your relationship, moving it from overdependence to healthy interdependence, allowing you to embrace the wise relationship.

appendix A

Tips for Nonanxious Partners

With this book in hand, both you and your partner hold the tools that can take your relationship to the next level. Each of you has taken a different path, however, to arrive at this same point. Your partner has learned and practiced new skills for handling his anxiety: time-outs, visualization exercises, and communication techniques. You, on the other hand, have been led to discover that you can't "fix" your partner's anxiety—and we encourage you not to try. Support and compassion, yes. Taking responsibility for it, no. You can, however, take responsibility for your own actions and interactions with your partner. There are many steps you can take that can help with this process.

Get informed. Learn about anxiety—its causes, its triggers, and its treatment. Part 1 of this book helped you understand the biological, genetic, and temperamental underpinnings of anxiety (see appendix D, "Resources," for additional sources of up-to-date information about anxiety). The more you understand the nature of anxiety, the easier it will be for you to be compassionate, understanding, and nonjudgmental.

Offer support in an affirming way. It can be difficult and frustrating at times to be in an intimate relationship with someone who is suffering from anxiety. Your partner's feelings may seem irrational, and your partner's behavior may seem both rigid and out of control. At these times, use the mirroring and validation skills from chapter 5 (along with the gratitude exercise from appendix B). Remember, you don't need to agree with your partner or even understand her perspective in order to validate her experience.

Affirm rather than enable. It can be tempting to feel that you need to fix or take care of your partner's anxiety by taking on extra roles and responsibilities in an effort to shield your partner from experiencing anxiety. Likewise, in the past you might have felt that you needed to always be "the rock," offering a steady source of emotional support for your partner while remaining unable to be vulnerable or get support yourself. As we wrote in chapter 4, only your partner has the power and the responsibility to reduce his own anxiety. Your support is invaluable, but if you take over for your partner, you are actively maintaining an overdependent bond.

Be optimistic and encouraging. There's a good chance that your partner underestimates her inner resources. Just knowing that you believe in and trust your partner can do wonders to help her gain much-needed confidence. There is tremendous value in being present for your partner in a caring and affirming way that simultaneously conveys your belief in your partner's ability to apply the tools in this book to regulate her anxiety. Even when your partner doubts that things will change, convey your optimism and positive expectancy that she has the strength to overcome anxiety.

Don't take on your partner's stress. Stress and anxiety can be contagious. Sometimes you might get nervous yourself when your partner is stressed. However, you can understand and empathize with your partner without becoming anxious yourself. The ongoing challenge is to maintain your emotional boundaries and yet be compassionate toward your partner.

Share decision making. Even if your partner wants you to take a large share of responsibility in decision making, encourage him to trust his own wisdom about decisions. Likewise, let your partner know that you trust that he can take risks and tolerate the distress that is sometimes a part of the decision-making process.

Acknowledge the positive changes. As your partner grows stronger and becomes more adept at regulating her anxiety, acknowledge and appreciate the positive changes you see. Likewise, as you notice improvements in your relationship, acknowledge and celebrate them as well. As you and your partner continue to engage in this process of repair, recovery, and discovery, you will have many opportunities to celebrate the new sense of intimacy and connection you are creating with the one you love.

Ask your partner for support. As your partner gets better at managing his anxiety, you can begin to ask for support from your partner when you are walking through a challenge. It's essential that you have the opportunity to both give and receive support—and the same holds true for your partner. Even when your partner is stressed, practicing the self-regulation strategies will help your partner shift his focus to you.

Acknowledge your own feelings. You may, at times, feel that your partner's emotions and thoughts are irrational or that your partner's behavior is rigid and out of control. At other times you may feel frustration, anger, or hurt. When these feelings come up, acknowledge them with acceptance and without judgment or self-recrimination. Having these feelings doesn't mean that you are unsupportive of your partner. Do, however, use the communication strategies in chapters 5 and 6 if you wish to share some of these feelings with your partner.

Find ways to relax. Meditation, relaxation exercises, calming audio CDs (see appendix D, "Resources," for a list of audio programs), and the daily stress inoculation are important for your well-being as well as your partner's. Doing the daily stress inoculation together, for example, can enhance your connection while simultaneously reinforcing your partner's self-soothing practice.

Be open to seeking professional help. Both individual and couples therapy can be a tremendous help to you. It's not a sign of weakness to seek out therapy. It is the wise person who recognizes the need for outside counsel and professional expertise. Just make sure the clinician you choose has training in the treatment of couples and anxiety disorders.

Use this book to enhance your partnership. As you read part 2 and began to engage in constructive communication with your partner, you gained another means to experience enhanced connection, care, and support. You can also consider asking your partner to share with you her experience of learning and implementing some of the exercises and techniques in this book. Sharing your experiences with each other as you each work to enrich your relationship will enhance your connection as well.

appendix B

Exercise for Nonanxious Partners—Soften Judgment, Access Appreciation

Living with a partner who is anxious can be difficult. You may, at times, feel bewildered, irritated, judgmental, or just plain exhausted when your partner's behavior appears irrational to you. These reactions are understandable, but they don't serve you or your partner. Luckily, you can learn to catch and shift your reactions when they pop up. Judgment, for instance, inevitably softens when you shift your focus to what you appreciate about your partner. The following exercise, which your partner and perhaps you practiced in chapter 6, can be especially helpful to you when you are emotionally triggered by your partner's heightened anxiety.

You can familiarize yourself with the exercise by reviewing the script a few times and then following it from memory. Or if you prefer, you can record the script, or have a friend or a therapist agree to read it to you. Then find a quiet, comfortable place where you won't be disturbed and begin.

Begin by positioning your body in a way that is most comfortable to you—taking as much time as you need to let yourself really settle in. And now, when you're ready, close your eyes and take a nice, deep breath in and hold it for a moment. Now release the breath with a long exhalation—and as you exhale, imagine that you are letting go of all tension, noticing how easy it is to focus on the breath, and let the breath move you into a different state of being—a more relaxed state of being. And now inhale and imagine that you are breathing in calmness, tranquility, and peace—with each cycle of breath taking you into a deeper and deeper state of calm. Continue to breathe slowly in this way, allowing yourself to feel more and more relaxed with each inhalation and exhalation.

Now that you are relaxed, take some time to enjoy what you most love about your partner—those qualities, those unique personal attributes that are precious to you—bringing to mind those characteristics, those actions, those parts of your partner's personality that you appreciate—that you admire, that you find wonderful. You might discover that even aspects of your partner's vulnerability or worried nature can be endearing. And as you allow each of these attributes to come into your mind, call to mind an image of your partner. Maybe it's a still image— your favorite picture. Or maybe it's more like a movie clip— allowing you to look in on your partner with a sense of warmth, care, and deep contentment, as you see your partner embodying the traits that you enjoy most.

And as you view this image of your partner—notice any sensations that arise in your body. Do you feel relaxed? Is there warmth in your hands or in your stomach? Perhaps you can notice just a hint of a smile on your face. And if there is no smile, perhaps you can create one—allowing the corners of your mouth to gently curl upward—as you enjoy all the endearing qualities of the one you love.

And to make it easier in the future for you to elicit these feelings of warmth and caring that you are sensing so powerfully right now, you can create a cue that will automatically give rise to these feelings at any time. To create this cue so that your mind and body activate these feelings, raise your right hand to your chest, gently placing the open palm of your hand over your heart. And as you rest your open palm over the place where your heart resides, sense the subtle, steady warmth that emanates from your core and collects in your open hand. And as you feel this warmth, call forth an image of your partner, an image that elicits all those endearing qualities that you appreciate. And hold this image for a minute or two, as you hold your hand to your heart, enjoying the calm contentment that this brings.

And with this cue, you are training your brain to very quickly push the replay button—so that these good feelings will come back automatically and quickly. So with this sensation of your hand over your heart, this cue, it will be very easy for you to elicit these soothing, calming, loving feelings of care, compassion, and regard. And you can gain a sense of relief in knowing that you can experience these feelings of compassion any time you wish, no matter what your partner is or isn't doing— allowing these calm and loving feelings to reemerge by bringing your right hand to your heart and tapping into this warm, soothing sense of care.

appendix C

Anxious in Love— The Book in Sixty Seconds

1. Know your triggers.

2. Take immediate time-outs as needed.

3. Practice the daily stress inoculation.

4. When you are triggered during interaction with your partner, take a time-out to self-soothe, honor your feelings, and validate your perspective.

5. Before initiating a difficult conversation, make sure both you and your partner are in a good mind-set.

6. Use your constructive communication tools (mirroring, validating, and empathizing) when you talk with your partner.

7. Maintain the goal of healthy interdependence.

8. Appreciate the wise, good-enough relationship.

9. Remember: practice makes permanent!

appendix D

Associations for Anxiety Disorders

The websites of the following associations, organizations, and foundations provide a plethora of resources and self-help suggestions.

Anxiety and Depression Association   adaa.org
of America

Anxieties.com   anxieties.com

National Alliance on Mental Illness   nami.org

Mindfulness Associates   mindfulnessassociates.com

Social Phobia/Social Anxiety   socialphobia.org
Association

Social Phobia World   socialphobiaworld.com

International OCD Foundation   ocfoundation.org

National Center for PTSD   www.ncptsd.va.gov

Books

Chronic Anxiety

Antony, Martin M., Michelle G. Craske, and David H. Barlow. 2006. *Mastering Your Fears and Phobias Workbook*. Treatments *That Work* series. 2nd ed. New York: Oxford University Press.

Antony, Martin M., and Peter J. Norton. 2009. *The Anti-Anxiety Workbook: Proven Strategies to Overcome Worry, Phobias, Panic, and Obsessions*. New York: The Guilford Press.

Bourne, Edmund J. 2010. *The Anxiety and Phobia Workbook*. 5th ed. Oakland, CA: New Harbinger Publications.

Burns, David D. 2006. *When Panic Attacks: The New, Drug-Free Anxiety Therapy That Can Change Your Life*. New York: Morgan Road Books.

Daitch, Carolyn. 2007. *Affect Regulation Toolbox: Practical and Effective Hypnotic Interventions for the Over-Reactive Client*. New York: W. W. Norton and Company.

——. 2011. *Anxiety Disorders: The Go-to Guide for Clients and Therapists*. New York: W. W. Norton and Company.

Davis, Martha, Elizabeth Robbins Eshelman, and Matthew McKay. 2008. *The Relaxation and Stress Reduction Workbook*. 6th ed. Oakland, CA: New Harbinger Publications.

Foa, Edna B., and Reid Wilson. 1991. *Stop Obsessing! How to Overcome Your Obsessions and Compulsions*. New York: Bantam Books.

Forsyth, John P., and Georg H. Eifert. 2007. *The Mindfulness and Acceptance Workbook for Anxiety: A Guide to Breaking Free from Anxiety, Phobias, and Worry Using Acceptance and Commitment Therapy*. Oakland, CA: New Harbinger Publications.

Hyman, Bruce M., and Cherry Pedrick. 1999. *The OCD Workbook: Your Guide to Breaking Free from Obsessive-Compulsive Disorder.* Oakland, CA: New Harbinger Publications.

Kabat-Zinn, Jon. 1991. *Full Catastrophe Living: Using the Wisdom of Your Body and Mind to Face Stress, Pain, and Illness.* New York: Delta.

Rothschild, Babette. 2011. *Trauma Essentials: The Go-To Guide.* New York: W. W. Norton and Company.

Wehrenberg, Margaret. 2008. *The 10 Best-Ever Anxiety Management Techniques: Understanding How Your Brain Makes You Anxious and What You Can Do to Change It.* New York: W. W. Norton and Company.

Wilson, Reid. 1996. *Don't Panic: Taking Control of Anxiety Attacks.* Rev. ed. New York: Harper Perennial.

Enhancing Your Relationship

Fruzzetti, Alan E. 2006. *The High-Conflict Couple: A Dialectical Behavior Therapy Guide to Finding Peace, Intimacy, and Validation.* Oakland, CA: New Harbinger Publications.

Gottman, John. 1994. *Why Marriages Succeed or Fail: And How You Can Make Yours Last.* New York: Fireside.

Gottman, John M., with Nan Silver. 1999. *The Seven Principles for Making Marriage Work: A Practical Guide from the Country's Foremost Relationship Expert.* New York: Three Rivers Press.

Hendrix, Harville. 1988. *Getting the Love You Want: A Guide for Couples.* New York: Henry Holt.

Hendrix, Harville, and Helen LaKelly Hunt. 2003. *Getting the Love You Want Workbook.* New York: Atria Books.

Zeig, Jeffrey, and Tami Kulbatski, eds. 2011. *Ten Commandments for Couples: For Every Aspect of Your Relationship Journey.* Phoenix, AZ: Zeig, Tucker, and Theisen.

Audio Programs

To order the audio programs by Carolyn Daitch, contact:

Center for the Treatment of Anxiety Disorders
E-mail: canxietydisorders@me.com
http://anxiety-treatment.com
http://anxietysolutionsonline

Daitch, Carolyn. 2003a. *Dialing Down Anxiety*. Audio CD. Farmington Hills, MI: Center for the Treatment of Anxiety Disorders. This audio program uses visualization, guided imagery, and established stress and anxiety-reduction techniques to counter the overreactions that accompany anxiety. anxietysolutionsonline.com.

————. 2003b. *The Insomnia Solution*. Audio CD and MP3. Farmington Hills, MI: Center for the Treatment of Anxiety Disorders. This audio program guides the listener into a relaxed state and the stillness of mind and body necessary for sleep. When you use it nightly, you can train your nervous system to elicit the appropriate level of relaxation to foster good sleep habits. anxiety-treatment.com.

————. 2009. *Alpha/Theta Sailing II*. Audio CD. Farmington Hills, MI: Center for the Treatment of Anxiety Disorders. This CD provides ambient music to promote a state of relaxation and well-being. Many use it as soothing background music at the office, at home, or while driving. This CD is especially useful for clients and clinicians who are using guided imagery, progressive relaxation, or hypnosis. When used in this context, it is designed to assist the listener in quickly moving into a state conducive to the development of therapist- or self-directed experience. anxiety-treatment.com.

————. 2010a. *Mastering Test Anxiety*. Audio CD. Farmington Hills, MI: Center for the Treatment of Anxiety Disorders. This recording is designed to help the listener master excessive anxiety over taking exams. It guides listeners to relax the nervous system while remaining alert and focused when preparing for and taking exams. anxietysolutionsonline.com.

———. 2010b. *Overcoming Emotional Eating: Breaking the Cycle of Stress- and Anxiety-Based Eating.* Audio CD. Waterford, MI: Mindfulness Associates. This audio program teaches the listener to discriminate between emotionally based cravings and real hunger. The program provides a set of tools to help the listener manage the stress, anxiety, and other emotions that lead to overeating. anxietysolutionsonline.com.

Naparstek, Belleruth. 1995. *Meditations to Relieve Stress.* Audio CD and MP3. Akron, OH: Health Journeys. This recording uses four exercises to help master anxiety and promote feelings of safety and protection. www.healthjourneys.com.

———. 2007. *Guided Meditations for Help with Panic Attacks.* Audio CD and MP3. Akron, OH: Health Journeys. This audio program uses healing imagery to reduce or eliminate acute anxiety and panic attacks. www.healthjourneys.com.

Yapko, Michael D. 2008. *Calm Down! A Self-Help Program for Managing Anxiety.* Audio CD and MP3. Fallbrook, CA: Yapko Publication. This audio program includes four CDs that teach self-hypnosis for reducing anxiety. www.yapko.com.

Resources for Professional Help

Selecting a Therapist and Treatment

Daitch, Carolyn. 2011. *Anxiety Disorders: The Go-to Guide for Clients and Therapists.* New York: W. W. Norton and Company. Guidance on finding and choosing a therapist and the treatment modalities that are right for you.

Cognitive Behavioral Therapy

Association for Behavioral and Cognitive   abct.org
Therapies (ABCT)

National Association of Cognitive-   nacbt.org
Behavioral Therapists (NACBT)

Relaxation Training

Benson-Henry Institute for Mind   www.massgeneral.org/bhi
Body Medicine

Mindfulness

Center for Mindfulness   www.umassmed.edu/cfm/index.aspx
in Medicine, Health
Care, and Society

Acceptance and Commitment Therapy (ACT)

Association for Contextual   contextualpsychology.org/act
Behavioral Science

Emotional Freedom Techniques (EFT)

World center for EFT   eftuniverse.com

Eye Movement Desensitization and Reprocessing (EMDR)

EMDR Institute	emdr.com
EMDR International Association (EMDRIA)	emdria.org

Hypnosis

American Society of Clinical Hypnosis (ASCH)	asch.net
Society for Clinical and Experimental Hypnosis (SCEH)	www.sceh.us
The Milton H. Erickson Foundation	erickson-foundation.org
The International Society of Hypnosis (ISH)	ish-hypnosis.org

References

Barlow, David H. 2002. *Anxiety and Its Disorders: The Nature and Treatment of Anxiety and Panic.* 2nd ed. New York: The Guilford Press.

Beattie, Melody. 1990. *The Language of Letting Go: Daily Meditations for Codependents.* San Francisco, CA: Harper and Row.

Billikopf Encina, Gregorio, 2006. "Listening Skills: Empathetic Approach—Listening First Aid," University of California, Berkeley, College of Natural Resources. Retrieved February 25, 2012. http://cnr.berkeley.edu/ucce50/ag-labor/7article/listening_skills.htm.

Coué, Emile. 1922. *The Coué "Method": Self Mastery through Conscious Autosuggestion.* Complete and Unabridged Ed. Translated by Archibald Stark van Orden. New York: Malkan Publishing.

Crowe, Cameron. 1996. *Jerry Maguire.* Directed by Cameron Crowe. Culver City, CA: TriStar Pictures and Gracie Films.

Daitch, Carolyn. 2007. *Affect Regulation Toolbox: Practical and Effective Hypnotic Interventions for the Over-Reactive Client.* New York: W. W. Norton and Company.

Emmons, Robert A., and Michael E. McCullough. 2003. "Counting Blessings versus Burdens: An Experimental Investigation of Gratitude and Subjective Well-Being in Daily Life." *Journal of Personality and Social Psychology* 84 (2):377-89.

Fruzzetti, Alan E. 2006. *The High-Conflict Couple: A Dialectical Behavior Therapy Guide to Finding Peace, Intimacy, and Validation.* Oakland, CA: New Harbinger Publications.

Goleman, Daniel. 2011. *The Brain and Emotional Intelligence: New Insights.* Northampton, MA: More than Sound LLC.

Gottman, John. 1994. *Why Marriages Succeed or Fail: And How You Can Make Yours Last.* New York: Fireside.

———. 2000. *Marital Therapy: A Research-Based Approach Training Seminar.* Training manual for participants of seminar, Couples Therapy: A Research-Based Approach—Level I Training, May. Novi, MI: The Gottman Institute.

Hendrix, Harville, and Helen Hunt. 1994. *The Couples Companion: Meditations and Exercises for Getting the Love You Want.* New York: Pocket Books.

Koneya, Mele, and Alton Barbour. 1976. *Louder Than Words: Nonverbal Communication.* Columbus, OH: Merrill.

LeDoux, Joseph. 1996. *The Emotional Brain: The Mysterious Underpinnings of Emotional Life.* New York: Simon and Schuster.

Luthe, Wolfgang, and Johannes H. Schultz. 1969. *Autogenic Therapy: Autogenic Methods.* Vol. 1. New York: Grune and Stratton.

Siegel, Daniel J. 2007. *The Mindful Brain: Reflection and Attunement in the Cultivation of Well-Being.* New York: W. W. Norton and Company.

Siegel, Daniel J. 2012. *The Developing Mind: How Relationships and the Brain Interact to Shape Who We Are.* 2nd ed. New York: Guilford Press.

Soussignan, Robert. 2002. "Duchenne Smile, Emotional Experience, and Autonomic Reactivity: A Test of the Facial Feedback Hypothesis." *Emotion* 2 (1):52–74.

Spiegel, Herbert, and David Spiegel. 1978. *Trance and Treatment: Clinical Uses of Hypnosis.* New York: Basic Books.

Winnicott, Donald. 1953. "Transitional Objects and Transitional Phenomena." *International Journal of Psychoanalysis* 34 (2):89–97.

Zajonc, Robert. 1985. "Emotion and Facial Efference: An Ignored Theory Reclaimed." *Science* 228 (4695):15–21.

Zajonc, Robert B., Sheila T. Murphy, and Marita Inglehart. 1989. "Feeling and Facial Efference: Implications of the Vascular Theory of Emotion." *Psychological Review* 96 (3):395–416.

Carolyn Daitch, PhD, is a licensed psychologist and certified Imago relationship therapist. She is the author of *Affect Regulation Toolbox* and *Anxiety Disorders: The Go-to Guide for Clients and Therapists.* She is also a contributing author in *Clinical Pearls of Wisdom: 21 Leading Therapists Offer Their Key Insights* and *Ten Commandments for Couples.* She specializes in treating anxiety disorders; trains health professionals internationally on hypnosis, anxiety disorders, affect regulation, and relationship therapy; and is the director of the Center for the Treatment of Anxiety Disorders in Farmington Hills, MI. Dr. Daitch lives in West Bloomfield, MI.

Lissah Lorberbaum, MA, holds a master's degree in clinical psychology with a specialization in somatic psychology and treats affect dysregulation across a wide range of clientele. She lives and works in Los Angeles, CA.

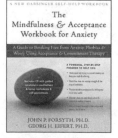
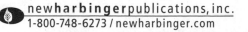

Real change *is* possible

For more than forty-five years, New Harbinger has published proven-effective self-help books and pioneering workbooks to help readers of all ages and backgrounds improve mental health and well-being, and achieve lasting personal growth. In addition, our spirituality books offer profound guidance for deepening awareness and cultivating healing, self-discovery, and fulfillment.

Founded by psychologist Matthew McKay and Patrick Fanning, New Harbinger is proud to be an independent, employee-owned company. Our books reflect our core values of integrity, innovation, commitment, sustainability, compassion, and trust. Written by leaders in the field and recommended by therapists worldwide, New Harbinger books are practical, accessible, and provide real tools for real change.

newharbingerpublications